WHERE DID JESUS GO?

Where Did Jesus Go?

The meaning and truth of the Resurrection

David Holloway

Marshalls

Marshalls Paperbacks
Marshall Morgan & Scott
3 Beggarwood Lane, Basingstoke, Hants., UK

Quotations from the Bible, unless otherwise stated are from the
Revised Standard Version, © 1952 and 1946.

ISBN 0 551 01051 7

Printed in Great Britain by
Richard Clay (The Chaucer Press) Ltd,
Bungay, Suffolk

For
Michael, Annabel and Zoë

Contents

Introduction

I once asked a student if he 'believed in Jesus Christ?' 'Oh, no!' he said, 'but I believe he rose from the dead. He was the first one that got away.'

This sort of conversation was predicted – by Jesus himself. He once said that the fact of someone rising from the dead would not necessarily convince people of the reality of God, of heaven or of hell. He implied that people would not necessarily be convinced about his own claims, even if *he* rose from the dead. But these claims and his resurrection have been believed by so many for so long that they can't be ignored. That some do not believe, is no excuse for not thinking about them.

Exactly what have Christians been saying all down the centuries? This: that one morning in a small 'buffer state' of the Roman Empire something was discovered of breath-taking proportions. Jesus of Nazareth had left the tomb. Subsequent evidence indicated that this was not like some other 'resurrections' that had taken place, or so it was said, on rare occasions in the history of the people of Israel, the Jews. This was different. The body of Jesus Christ had not only emerged from the tomb, but it was transformed. It was, and it was not, the old body.

Is this believable? Ever since the tomb was found to be empty people have denied the Resurrection. The enemies of the disciples said that the body was stolen. This did not then and has not since carried conviction as an explanation. Some have tried to escape the challenge of the resurrection of Jesus by laughing it off. Some of the city fathers and philosophers in Athens in Paul's day tried to do that. 'When they heard of the resurrection of the dead, some mocked' (Acts 17.32). Voltaire, several centuries later, used his wit to the same effect. In one of his stories he makes the Phoenix say to the Princess of Babylon: 'Resurrection, madam, is one of the most simple things in the world . . . Everything in this world is the effect of resurrection; caterpillars are regenerated into butterflies; a kernel put into the earth is regenerated into a tree. All animals buried in the earth regenerate into vegetations, herbs and plants, and nourish other animals . . .'

But you can't laugh the Resurrection away. You've got to give an account for that 'one morning' when the tomb was found empty.

The basic questions must be answered: what happened; why did it happen if it did; if it did happen why was it, and why is it, difficult for some to believe; and what does it mean for us today?

It is these sorts of questions that this book is going to consider. These are *the* questions for the Church in any age, and therefore for the Church in *this* age. The Church was founded on the belief that Jesus rose and left the tomb. Christians like Stephen in the New Testament, Polycarp a little later, other saints and martyrs over the centuries, men like Dietrich Bonhoeffer under the Nazis and countless others under Communist and Fascist regimes in our own day have given their lives because they believed that Jesus Christ rose from the dead and there is a life beyond the stoning, the stake or the scaffold. Bonhoeffer said, as he was going out to be executed by the Nazis: 'This is the end, but for me the beginning of life.' What confidence! But is such a faith *always* the property of those who call themselves 'Christian'?

Writing to a young Christian leader, and a friend, Paul had this to say: 'Remember Jesus Christ, risen from the dead' (2 Tim. 2.8). It's amazing how Christians can forget or neglect the Resurrection. I was in a library of a distinguished Theological Seminary in the United States recently. Out of 123,000 volumes there were only a few hundred on the Resurrection. Nor can I point the finger. When I was first asked to write a book on the Resurrection, I immediately thought of all the other books I wanted to write – on the nature of Scripture, on Christian social ethics, on church growth and church management and so on. The truth dawned on me, however – a truth I had long known – that all these are so much 'hot air' unless Jesus rose from the dead. As the New Testament puts it bluntly and unambiguously,

'If Christ has not been raised, your faith is futile' (1 Cor. 15.17). I therefore had to write this book.

The book is for those who do not yet believe in Christ or his resurrection. It is to help them think through the issues. It is also for those who do believe, to remind them of what is central to their faith.

We all live in a modern complex world. We all can be so absorbed with the problems of the present that we neglect the fundamental issues. Basic questions have first to be answered before we can solve the many problems of the present: Why am I here? Where am I going? What happens after death? – all questions related to the one question that is the focus of this book, *Where did Jesus go?*

David Holloway
Jesmond Parish Church
Newcastle upon Tyne

1: Miracles, science and the modern world

Setting the scene – a parable

Alan, a young man in his mid-twenties, and Rachel, a girl of about the same age, left a suburban house one evening. 'I didn't agree with a lot of that,' Alan said. 'Anyhow,' he continued as they walked along, 'I'd rather talk about us!'

A little later Miriam, an older woman, left the same house. She was with her sister. A headmistress, she was active in local affairs. Soon after leaving she commented, 'It was all very interesting, but I'm still not convinced.'

Timothy was yet another person to leave the house. 'I'm very confused,' he said to David, as they waited at the bus stop. David, a colleague at work, had invited him along; so he felt a bit disappointed.

What had been going on?

The local church was holding a series of house meetings, and each week for four weeks a different topic was being discussed. The topic for that evening had been 'The resurrection of Jesus'. Eight people had been present at this meeting. Alan, Miriam and Timothy were the 'guests' and not card-carrying Christians, while the other five were regular church members.

The meeting had begun with a tape-recorded introduction by the minister. 'Our subject for tonight's house meetings,' he began, 'is the central event of the Christian faith. The world was turned upside down when people started to believe in it. I'm talking about the resurrection of Jesus of Nazareth.' There was a pause . . . 'What set things going was the announcement of a simple fact, a simple fact anyone could check: *a tomb was empty*. The importance of this mustn't be forgotten. "It is always possible (he was obviously reading from a book) to find an ingenious explanation for the impressions of events that men and women take away with them. Perhaps they are subject to delusions, or they are poor observers, or they jump to conclusions; but an empty grave is a cold blooded affair which remains in its same condition of emptiness whatever the emotional stress of the onlookers. Joseph of Arimathea's vacant grave with its massive stone door rolled aside stood as a silent witness to the world that something strange had happened."[1] Tonight, then,' he concluded, 'you're going to be discussing what is at the heart of Christianity, the Resurrection. Your starting question is simply this: '*Where did Jesus go?*' I hope all the groups have a good time.' And with that he signed off.

After a short silence Rachel started the ball rolling. 'I believe that Jesus went to his Father after his resurrection.' 'What on earth does that mean?' said Alan. A whole host of questions were then raised. 'Yes, but don't we have to say that Jesus went out into the world?' said Miriam's sister. She felt that what was being said about the ascension of Jesus was not very helpful. 'When Christians are filled with the Holy Spirit aren't they 'Jesus Christ' in the world?' The discussion moved on to a new tack.

After a time Timothy decided he wanted to steer things in yet another direction. 'Do you think,' he asked, 'we could discuss the real issues – miracles, science and that sort of thing? How is it possible for someone to rise from the dead? Some people can believe anything. Cranks and religion often go together. I was reading in the paper about this man who thought he was the Messiah and tried to walk on the sea. The only trouble was he couldn't swim.' The others laughed. 'It wasn't funny – he drowned. I'm not kidding. It was true.'[2] 'Well, I'd like to talk a bit about the other religions,' said Alan. 'Don't they all go in for "resurrections"?'

The discussion was quite stimulating. No one seemed to have been bored, whatever their views. They agreed to have an 'extra' meeting. Before this one, though, they would all try to read a book about the resurrection of Jesus

The Miraculous

That little suburban house meeting, which could have happened anywhere, was focusing on the key questions.

So let's start right away with one of the questions – that about miracles.

Many people believe that the *real* problems about the Resurrection all have to do with 'miracles' and 'science'. 'How is it possible for someone to rise from the dead? Some people can believe anything.' That was Timothy's position in the house meeting.

Has science proved that 'miracles' can't happen? There are still a lot of people who believe it has. 'Nature is entirely predictable,' they say. 'What happens in nature can be discovered by able men and women in universities and research establishments. If certain things baffle us at the moment, it is only a matter of time before all will be made clear. But what is now clear is that miracles don't happen and people certainly don't rise from the dead.'

A playboy socialite from Edinburgh held this view a couple of hundred years ago. His name was David Hume. It was just when modern science was beginning to develop. Although he was equally as happy with the high life of those days as with writing essays and books, he managed to give time to writing extensively on philosophical subjects. His books on these have been of lasting influence. In one of them he gave 'classic' expression to this belief in science and disbelief in miracles. 'A miracle,' he wrote, 'is a violation of the laws of nature; and as a firm and unalterable experience has established these laws, the proof against a miracle, from the very nature of the fact, is as entire as any argument from experience can possibly be imagined.'[3]

A lot, however, has changed in the last two hundred years, with a lot changing very recently. The bubble of scientific confidence is on the point of bursting. Christopher Booker reckons it *has* burst. The scientific dream is no longer with us – the dream that through scientific discovery and invention all the 'secrets of the universe' can be unlocked, the dream that in time all of us will be able to live lives of unfettered comfort and ease. He argues that as we move into the last decades of the twentieth century we have passed beyond 'a profoundly significant moment . . . in the history of mankind – the moment when it became apparent that, even on their own terms, science and technology were no longer necessarily making life better, easier, more efficient for us all.'[4]

We needn't bother with the reasons for this. Perhaps an uncontrolled desire for material things has caused it – a desire that leads to economic stress on a universal scale, with problems for rich and poor alike. Perhaps the abuse of science is a cause. One of the first secretaries of the Royal Society when it was founded as a scientific institution was a bishop. He would have been horrified at the use of science for mass destruction and environmental pollution!

Whatever the cause, there does seem to be a shift of mood and belief and, indeed, there are quite radical developments in some quarters. People are no longer confident about the physical universe in the way Hume used to be. Perhaps the world is more strange than we thought. However bizarre it may seem, some are fusing mysticism and science. They believe that the world of 'spirit' can affect the world of 'matter'. This thinking has more to do with Eastern Religion than Christianity, but it is a serious development. In his book *Mysticism and the New Physics* Michael Talbot has claimed that the old certainties have now gone. 'Slowly,' he says, 'the tremendous mass of the scientific establishment begins to feel the first tremors of a radical and awesome new age. . . Perhaps the change will be felt like a roll of thunder as old constructions fall and new ones take their place. Perhaps the change will be so subtle and gradual that we will have no more sense of it than the anti-Copernicans during the lifetime of Galileo, who did not feel the earth move. Whatever the case, the message of the new physics is that we are participators in a universe of ever-increasing wonder.'[5]

None of this solves the problems that people like Timothy have. It just makes them all the more bewildered. What does the 'new physics' have to say about the Resurrection? Very little. But it means that at last people are prepared to give the resurrection of Jesus a fair hearing, or some are! In the past there has often been what James Martin calls 'a deep-rooted prejudice against belief in the Resurrection.' This has affected many people. 'Dominated by the modern mind, they find it well-nigh impossible to think of the Resurrection as a real possibility. Miracles, they are sure, do not happen, cannot happen, never did happen. Therefore the Resurrection cannot be true.'[6]

But a wind of change is blowing.

The limits of science

What can science tell us? Natural Science – physics, chemistry, biology etc. – has been very important for all of us in the modern world. True, the world today may be confused. *Time* magazine once described Britain, the place where modern science grew up, as 'adrift in a deepening crisis of faith.' But no one would want to lose all the real advantages won by science and technology over the last centuries and during the twentieth century in particular. Indeed, we could now be faced with a reaction. Today there is a danger of going to the other extreme, as there is a fascination, for many, with the irrational and the uncanny. That is leading to 'a revolt of the soul against the intellect' – to use W. B. Yates's phrase.

But the Christian isn't over impressed with that reaction. The Christian believes in a rational, orderly universe that science can investigate. He or she finds no problem in its stability. In one sense it is only against such a background that miracles can occur. A miracle can be contrasted with the apparently normal only because there *is* a normal, orderly pattern to the universe's working. In the words of God as reported in Genesis, 'While the earth remains, seedtime and harvest, cold and heat, summer and winter, day and night, shall not cease' (Gen. 8.22).

The problems over science arise only when our thinking about the material universe colours our thinking about the whole of the life of man. Why, for example, should man and society be likened either to the planets or to the machines of human invention? Over the centuries this has happened. The scientific mind elated with its successes in the non-human world has often, unwittingly, treated man as non-human. Man has gradually been seen as a miniature universe – a mass of interconnected laws of cause and effect, or as a sophisticated machine. But, of course, men are not miniature universes or machines. They are very different.

The reason why the natural sciences were so successful was because 'nature' or the universe of physical laws has been easier to understand and control than *human* nature. Human nature is very different and much harder to understand and control. It is easier to send space craft round Jupiter and Saturn than it is to solve the problems of East and West, Arab and Jew, rich and poor, or the violence on the streets of any major big city! That is why science has evolved the way it has with a huge success-rate in its investigation of the physical world.

But we need to remember the story of the man in the street at night looking down at the pavement under a lamp-post. 'What are you doing?' he was asked. 'I've lost my frontdoor key,' he replied. 'Are you sure you've lost it under the lamp-post?' 'No, but this is the only place where I can see!'

We must be careful, therefore, before we look for the key to human life with the lamp of science; perhaps we need another lamp. In his 'Gifford Lectures' the German physicist and philosopher C. F. von Weizäcker put it like this: 'Science cannot select the order in which it wants to treat its subjects according to their importance for human life. The motion of the planets is not relevant to human happiness or salvation. But it turned out to be a comparatively simple problem for mathematical treatment, and thus through the efforts of Copernicus, Kepler, and Newton its theory became the keystone of modern science. Human nature is less simple.'[7]

Man has a free will. That is what makes the difference. Although subject to environmental and hereditary factors, man can act creatively on his own. He is not totally determined, nor is he a robot.

But it has to be admitted some disagree. 'Can *we* really determine,' they say, 'even a small part of the universe? Even when we think we are acting freely, how can we be sure?'

Part of the answer will come as we look at the resurrection of Jesus. If the tomb was empty, if he really rose from the dead, if God is 'there', man is certainly not just a 'throw-up' of the physical universe. God is ultimate. His is the last word, not the laws of an impersonal universe. Man is then in his image and thus a free creative being.

How important that we discover the truth about the resurrection of Jesus! To do that we need to look at facts, not theories.

Miracles in the New Testament

We face a paradox in the New Testament over the miracles of Jesus. On the one hand, just to take Mark's gospel alone, we find a great deal about miracles. Thirty-one per cent of the Gospel, 209 out of 666 verses, is taken up with miracle stories. In the early chapters it is forty-seven per cent. 'St Mark without miracle is indeed Hamlet without the Prince.'[8]

On the other hand, for all that is said about the miracles of Jesus, there is a desire to play them down. For example, when Jesus once healed a leper, he said to the man, 'See that you say nothing to anyone' (Mark 1.44).

Jesus was aware that his miracles, or 'signs' as John prefers to call them, would be misunderstood. They did not have 'evidential' value; rather they were the result of his love in the face of suffering. By themselves apart from his total teaching they could mislead people. As a result of a miracle on one occasion the Jews tried to make Jesus a powerful political leader; they wanted to make him a king. There had just been a miraculous feeding of five thousand people and the conclusion drawn was: 'This is indeed the prophet who is to come into the world' (John 6.14). But the miracle misled them. They had wrong ideas about the sort of person and the sort of job that 'the prophet' was to have. 'Miracle' was only part of the story.

The miracles of the New Testament can only be viewed in the light of the Old Testament and its understanding of God and the universe. Here the important thing to remember is that the Hebrews were so different to the Greeks and many of us today!

Basically the Greeks (and their successors) tried first of all to make sure of 'nature'; and when that was done, they fitted God in. The Hebrews, as we can see from the Old Testament, went about it the other way round. They first tried to make sure of God, and then saw where 'nature' fitted in. They did not think of a closed, self-sufficient universe or system of 'nature'. In fact they hardly thought in terms of 'nature' at all. God's word and his will were what they were concerned with. For example, spring follows winter and summer follows spring in response to God's command, not in obedience to 'natural laws'.

The ancient Israelite believed in regularity just as much as his

Greek counterpart. But for him it is regularity in the character of God, not a purely physical regularity; he knew the character of God to be consistent and true to his word.

For this reason in the Bible miracles are not seen as bizarre, irrational interventions from outside. That was more of a pagan view, not a Christian one. Rather they are seen to be consistent with the justice and love of God, and so as we would expect there is a restraint about the reporting of them. This immediately separates them off from many other reported miracles, ancient and modern.

A God-centred universe

Plutarch was a priest of the Greek god, Apollo, and an exact contemporary of Mark; but the miracles they write about are so different.

In one of his works Plutarch tells about the Greek general, Pyrrhus (of 'Pyrrhic victory' fame).[9] He mentions how once the general was involved in a sacrifice, when suddenly the severed heads of the oxen that had been killed stuck out their tongues. They then began to lick up their own blood! Plutarch describes this as 'a remarkable portent' or (literally) 'a great sign'. It is inconceivable that that sort of thing could have been one of the 'signs' of Jesus.

It cannot be too often said: the biblical miracles are not to be seen as 'suspensions of natural laws'. For some have seen God as the great 'clockmaker', who puts the world together, winds it up and then lets it tick. From time to time he presses the 'stop' button and 'does a miracle'. No! The Bible's view is that God created and *still* sustains the world. There is a permanent, continuing relationship between God and what we call the material universe. In fact it is Jesus Christ himself, according to the New Testament, who is the 'agent' in this process. 'In him all things hold together' (Col. 1.17). That was Paul's staggering assertion. The writer of the epistle to the Hebrews said that he 'upholds the universe by his word of power' (Heb. 1.3). Jesus Christ is at the heart of the universe – or so those early Christians believed. If that is true, the Resurrection far from being odd is what you might expect!

So to recap, in the Bible the material universe within which the 'miraculous' takes place is all part of God's realm and in part it reflects his character. 'The heavens are telling the glory of God; and the firmament proclaims his handiwork' is how the Psalmist put it (Ps. 19.1). That is why the ultimate principle of order and regularity is to be seen not in the physical universe, but in the God who is the creator of that universe. 'The only ultimate regularity,' writes C. F. D. Moule, 'is to be looked for not within the material realm by itself but in the character of a personal God. It is of his character that the material realm is a manifestation: and what is possible and probable in it is better measured by what is known of the character of God than by what is observed on the much narrower scale of the purely mechanistic.'[13]

When we look at Jesus, we see, says the Christian, the character of God. 'He who has seen me has seen the Father,' said Jesus (John 14.9). And what we find to be true of Jesus may have to make us revise our ideas of 'the possible'.

A miracle therefore is not so much an intervention or a suspension of natural law; rather it is what happens when the love and goodness of God is directed in an intense way at the imperfections of nature. God's activity in nature and history is 'focused to burning-point' in miracle.

And that is why the miracle stories of the Apocryphal literature have to be rejected. As we shall see, they are often so out of keeping with the character of Jesus. But the resurrection of Jesus is a very different matter.

We shall never be able to get away from the 'miraculous' in Christianity. In fact it is a distinguishing mark of the Christian faith as compared with some of the other main religions. Yes, in some popular forms of other religions there is a belief in miracles. But Confucius was not a miraculous figure. The Buddha allowed only 'the miracles of the revelation of man's inner self;[11] for him it is in knowledge that the miraculous is to be found. Muhammad also disclaimed the power to work miracles; the Qur'ān alone was miraculous.

And remember: the strongest evidence for the miracles of Jesus comes from his enemies. They objected to his works of power. But in the New Testament there is no indication that they generally denied them. True, when Jesus healed a man born blind, the Jews at first were reluctant to believe that this had really happened. John tells us: 'The Jews did not believe that he had been born blind and had received his sight, *until* they called the parents of the man who had received his sight, and asked them, "Is this your son, who you say was born blind?" ' (John 9.18–19). They were then forced to accept the facts. In the end they had to admit the healing and the power of Jesus.

Conclusion

So we mustn't be prejudiced by some assumptions people easily can have about science and miracles. We need, instead, to see how the Bible understands the 'miraculous'. In the light of that we need to think about the resurrection of Jesus Christ.

2: The issues involved

Bertrand Russell

Bertrand Russell was an 'enfant terrible' of the earlier part of the twentieth century. Before the second World War he gained some notoriety for his views on sexual behaviour. He was one of the forerunners of the permissive society. 'I developed the view,' he tells us, 'that complete fidelity was not to be expected in most marriages.'[1] But he not only threw overboard Christian personal and sexual ethics, he also jettisoned Christian beliefs about God and Jesus Christ. His book *Why I am not a Christian* shows us his position – a position that had no room for the resurrection of Jesus Christ.

For many in the Western world of the twentieth century he symbolised and summed up their own attitudes and ideas. He was able to give expression to these in a way few could imitate. Listen to how he soliloquises on the meaning of life and the universe. It is a brilliant description of despair. 'The mental night that has descended upon me is less brief and promises no awakening after sleep. Formerly the cruelty, the meanness, the dusty fretful passion of human life seemed to me a little thing, set, like some resolved discord in music, amid the splendour of the stars and the stately procession of geological ages. What if the universe was to end in universal death; it was none the less unruffled and magnificent. But now all this has shrunk to be no more than my own reflection in the windows of the soul, through which I look out upon the night of nothingness.

The revolutions of nebulae, the birth and death of stars, were no more than convenient fictions in the trivial work of linking together my own sensations, and perhaps those of other men not much better than myself. No dungeon was ever constructed so dark and narrow as that in which the shadow physics of our time imprisons us; for every prisoner has believed that outside his walls a free world existed; but now the prison has become the whole universe. There is darkness without and when I die there will be darkness within. There is no splendour, no vastness, anywhere; only triviality for a moment, and then nothing.'[2]

I shall never forget one occasion when it seemed right to read that passage in public. I was on a university mission in Oxford when over the radio we heard of the death of Bertrand Russell. After a very long life the old philosopher and anti-nuclear campaigner was no more. It was a sad moment. David MacInnes from Birmingham was the main missioner on the mission team. So I suggested to him that he should read this passage from the *Autobiography* during his address that night. The Union Debating chamber was packed. There was an 'overflow' meeting to a nearby hall. Hundreds of students were present, and most had by now heard of Russell's death.

As the passage was read out there was total silence. Here was a man who had died without God and without hope and who had turned his back on the resurrection of Jesus Christ from the dead. The contrast between the glorious hope of Jesus and the Resurrection being preached that night and the total despair of Bertrand Russell could almost be felt.

Hope and forgiveness

Contrast that with the situation of another man. He was from Alaska and in the world's terms, unlike Russell, insignificant. He had a bad home. The only friendship he ever experienced was from a Christian school teacher. Many years after he left school, the teacher received a letter. The gist of it was this: 'Dear Teacher, You may not remember me; but I've now got an ugly story. I'm in death row awaiting execution for murder.'

The letter went on like this: 'I desire to die so that is OK; but one thing bothers me. I'm afraid of what comes after death. I know you believe in God and prayer, and that is why I ask your help now. In other words, I cannot face what lies beyond with guilt on my soul and no hope of forgiveness. If you still believe in God, write and give me the courage to face death.'

The teacher then entered into correspondence. She spoke of the death of Christ on the cross and how he had borne the penalty for human sin as she believed. Then she made a positive suggestion. He should take a big sheet of paper and write down all his crimes, fears, sins and hatreds and say, 'God, here it all is – all of it. Forgive me, Father' and then destroy the paper.

The result was another letter: 'Dear Teacher, I followed your instructions perfectly. I want you to know – because you love me regardless of everything. I stayed on my knees all night praying. I wasn't conscious of time or anything, only of God's forgiveness and love pouring over my guilty soul.

When the guard came with breakfast I lay on the floor as though dead. The man stared at me, turned white and fear showed in his eyes. "You OK?" he choked out. I nodded and smiled. The guard looked at me again. "My God," he gasped, "there's a light on your face." He set the tray down and fled.

Through God's grace I am clean, clean. I could shout it from the house tops . . . I'm not afraid anymore of death or the hereafter. I am condemned to die in the gas chamber. I am ready. God is with me. . . All is well, strong and sure. I go forth to meet my God.'

Compared with Bertrand Russell here was a man humanly insignificant. But he was a man with a sure and certain hope as he prepared for death. And it was the resurrection of Jesus that gave him assurance of *forgiveness* as well as hope.

Jesus himself implied that the Resurrection and forgiveness go together. Before his disciples had much idea about the Resurrection or even his death, Jesus began to make them think about the question we have set ourselves, the question about *where Jesus was going to*. His remarks were enigmatic, but later they were seen to have been providing clues about the *meaning* as well as the destination of his journey.

Think back to that occasion when the disciples were in the upper room the evening before the Crucifixion. Jesus had washed their feet – a remarkable sign of humility and service. Judas had gone out into the night. And Jesus then said, 'I am going to him who sent me' (John 16.5) and went on to speak about the Holy Spirit. He said that the Holy Spirit would come to them, when he left, and would 'convince the world' on issues such as sin, righteousness and judgment. But the conviction of the world over 'righteousness' would be directly related to where Jesus was going: 'the Counsellor will . . . convince the world . . . concerning righteousness, *because I go to the Father*, and you will see me no more' (John 16.10).

No doubt this was as confusing to those disciples as it is today to anyone not familiar with the events that followed. But after the resurrection of Jesus the disciples came to see precisely what it meant.

It meant that the resurrection of Jesus from the tomb was God's 'Yes' to his death on the cross. To them it proved that on the cross Christ had borne the world's sin and guilt – and that included theirs. Christ's death was not a criminal's punishment, even though some thought judicial crucifixion could only be that. The Resurrection proved the 'rightness' of Christ. So his death had to be something very different. In time it was seen as God's way of enabling them to be 'right' with him and forgiven. Paul summarised this when he said: 'Jesus our Lord . . . was put to death for our trespasses and raised for our justification (lit. "to establish our justification")' (Rom. 4.25). And this is what that man in Alaska believed.

But was it all wishful thinking? Did Jesus really go anywhere apart from into the ground?

The apostolic preaching – not the immortality of the soul

Before we can begin to answer those questions we must know what it was that the early Christians were saying about the Resurrection.

We start with one certain fact. The early Christians were saying and believing that something had happened. And what had happened meant that death was no longer to be feared. They believed that Jesus Christ had gone to his Father so that 'through death he might destroy him who has the power of death, that is the devil, and deliver all those who through fear of death were subject to lifelong bondage' (Heb. 2.14–15). Then as now there were more people afraid of death than probably cared to admit it. But the Christians were different. They were so confident that death had not held Jesus that they believed it would not hold them either. The apostolic preaching and teaching makes this clear.

There is a simple statement of the essence of that teaching in the Acts of the Apostles. We find it where we read about the embarrassment the preaching of the Christians caused 'the establishment'. The authorities were 'annoyed because they were teaching the people and proclaiming *in Jesus the resurrection from the dead*' (Acts 4.2).

Here you have it. They were preaching 'in Jesus the resurrection from the dead.' But what does that really mean? First, perhaps, we need to ask what it does *not* mean?

The resurrection from the dead did not and does not mean the immortality of the soul on its own. In New Testament times there were quite a number of people who believed that, as in the case of John Brown, the soul 'goes marching on'. The Greek philosopher Plato had influenced the world with his teaching on the immortality of the soul. Many subsequently had accepted his views. When his mentor, Socrates, had been forced to drink hemlock and died, Plato believed his soul had at last escaped from his body where it had been entombed. Plato and his school even tried to connect the Greek word for a 'body', *sōma*, with the Greek word for a 'tomb', *sēma*. He tried to say that the body is really a 'tomb' or 'death cell' of the 'soul' or 'spirit'.

These views had been adopted by some within Judaism. Josephus, a first century Jewish historian, tells us of one group within Judaism who 'believe that souls have power to survive death and that there are rewards and punishment under the earth for those who have led lives of virtue and vice: eternal imprisonment is the lot of evil souls, while the good souls receive an easy passage to a new life.'[3] But the main thrust of the Bible and certainly the teaching of the Apostles in the New Testament is very much against the immortality of the soul by itself. Nor does it see the soul as inherently good while the body is evil.

The assumption behind Plato's view is that matter is evil. The Christian says, 'Nonsense! Matter is good.' If you're in doubt go back to those early chapters of Genesis. No matter how you view them, one message rings out loud and clear: 'creation is good.' You have it in the refrain, 'God saw that it was good . . . God saw that it was good.' At each stage of the creation of the material universe this refrain comes in. Yes, the universe as we experience it is 'fallen'. The world as it is is not the world as it ought to be. But the Bible makes it quite clear that the 'fall' is not the act of 'creation'. The fall comes *after* the creation as those early chapters of the Bible make it clear. The evil in the world is not to be thought of as being there originally. Sin and selfishness come after the 'beginning' and then cause evil.

In the early centuries of the Christian church and even during the period of the preaching of the Apostles there were those on the 'fringes' of the Christian community who tried to deny all this. We know them as the 'Gnostics'; and we now have a particularly good idea of what they said and believed. A remarkable find of their writings was dug up from the soil of Nag Hammadi in Upper Egypt in 1945. But even before that from the perhaps biased reports of their critics we had a reasonable idea of their main tenets. They argued that suffering, toil, pain and death were all part of the original creation. Like Aldous Huxley in modern times, they saw the creation as part of an 'aboriginal calamity'. And the Gnostics insisted on the immortality of the soul, while denying the value of bodies and the material world. For example in a *Treatise on Resurrection* that has been recovered from Nag Hammadi, a person called Rheginos is told that he ought to think that 'the world is an apparition'.[4]

Resurrection – not resuscitation

So when the Apostles preached 'in Jesus the resurrection from the dead', they were certainly not meaning by that an immortality of the soul. Equally they were not meaning the 'resuscitation of the body'. They did not mean, in crude terms, that the old bits came together again just as before.

Some people who overheard the Apostles' preaching may not have realised that at first. They may have tied in this new teaching on 'resurrection' with what they remembered from one of their own sacred writings. In one of the books of the Apocrypha we can read of Razis, a Jewish leader from an earlier period; he committed suicide by taking a sword and disembowelling himself after he had failed to kill himself outright. 'Standing on a sheer rock, and now completely drained of blood, he took his entrails in both hands and flung them at the crowd. And thus, invoking the Lord of life and breath *to give these entrails back to him again*, he died' (NEB 2 Maccabees 14.46).

Such a gruesome story of Razis praying for a physical resuscitation may have stuck in the minds of some. This may have lead some of those listening to the Apostles to think of the Resurrection in terms of Jesus being 'reformed' just as before. This would be a parallel to those raisings of the dead we read of during Jesus' earthly ministry. It was reported that the son of a widow from Nain came back to life (Luke 7.11–15), that the daughter of a Jewish official called Jairus came back to life (Mark 5.22–42) and that the same thing happened in the case of Jesus' friend, Lazarus (John 11.1–44). But of course such people were raised simply to normal human life again, not to full resurrection life. Presumably they died subsequently in old age or before. There are reports of similar instances in the Old Testament. Elijah was involved in bringing a boy back to life, as was Elisha (1 Kings 17.17–24; 2 Kings 4.18–37).

But the resurrection of Jesus is not spoken of as a resuscitation of a corpse. No, it was the resurrection to new bodily possibilities. It was a bodily transformation, not a resuscitation. If it really happened it is immediately good news for all those physically or mentally handicapped in this life. So much is at stake here.

The stakes were nowhere clearer than in the mid-sixties. J. B. Phillips tells us that it was then that 'a clergyman, old, retired, useless if you like, took his own life because some well-fed, prosperous, popular professor of theology spoke so convincingly on the "telly", that the parson in his loneliness and ill-health concluded that his whole life's work had been founded upon a lie. Jesus Christ did not really rise from the dead, according to the learned professor, and the New Testament could no longer be regarded as reliable history.'[5]

A little later another professor of theology appeared on British Television, Professor Geoffrey Lampe of Cambridge. He was preaching a televised sermon on Easter Day 1965 from St Martin's, Birmingham Parish Church. In his sermon he had this to say of Christ: 'He remains buried. The real Christ is not a revived corpse.'[6] In a discussion on television that same evening, when six people questioned Professor Lampe about his views and the sermon they had heard earlier in the day, he said this: 'I regard the story of the empty tomb as a myth.'[7] Enormous controversy followed.

It may be worth asking at this point why did Professor Lampe believe what he did? Was it *really* that the New Testament texts about the empty tomb were now discredited by scholarship? No.

In an informal seminar at Cambridge when I questioned him on his beliefs, he replied that it was the experiences of life that made him think as he did. He told of what had happened in the second World War. A friend was blown to pieces in a tank. 'I had to bury him; but all that was left of him was a foot,' he said; 'What sense can you make of the resurrection of the *body* after that?' But surely that begs the question. 'Resurrection' is not 'resuscitation'.

Ironically at the same time as theologians at Cambridge were saying these sorts of things, secular philosophers at Oxford were saying that the notion of survival in a future life could only be made sense of logically by *bodily* resurrection. They did not all believe in it, by any means. But as the philosopher Professor Sir Peter Strawson wrote: 'No doubt it is for this reason that the orthodox have wisely insisted on the resurrection of the body.'[8]

The body went

The fiercest critics of the early Christians, we are told, admitted that the tomb was empty. They countered this fact not by saying that it was all a myth; rather they said the disciples had stolen the body (Matt. 28.13). But the disciples who knew that that wasn't true said, 'No. Jesus has risen and left the tomb.'

For the moment we are not concerned with the evidence for this claim. We just need to make sure we know what this claim was. It was that Jesus had been raised and the tomb was now vacant.

The New Testament clearly records a *bodily* resurrection, but the body had new characteristics. It seemed to have new powers. This was a 'glorified' body, or, to use the slightly confusing New Testament term, a 'spiritual' body.

Look at what it was like! The Gospels show that the resurrection body of Jesus could be touched and seen (Matt. 28.9; John

20.17, 27) and his voice could be heard (John 20.16). The resurrection appearances of Jesus were certainly not those of a disembodied spirit (Luke 24.39, 42–3). By eating fish in the disciples' presence, Jesus demonstrated to them the 'reality' of his resurrection state. But then Jesus had the power to appear and disappear at will.

Here were the disciples cowering together behind locked doors. Suddenly Jesus appeared to them (John 20.19–26). On another occasion two disciples met Jesus as they were going on a short journey out of town to a small place called Emmaus. At first they did not recognise him. The truth dawned only when they had a meal together. But he then suddenly vanished out of their sight (Luke 24.13–31).

And then there is the stone. The stone door to the rock tomb also tells us something of the nature of Jesus resurrection body. Remember, it was rolled away from the tomb to let the disciples see and go in. It was not rolled away to let Jesus out. That is never suggested.

The empty tomb is an important clue to the nature of the resurrection body of Jesus. *It is not that the empty tomb proves the Resurrection*. Rather it proves what sort of resurrection it was, *if* it took place.

Indeed the gospel narratives are quite clear that the empty tomb did not generally suggest the Resurrection. Mark tells us that the women who first went to the tomb and found it empty were terrified (Mark 16.8). The two disciples on their way to Emmaus knew about the empty tomb (Luke 24.22–4), but had no ideas of resurrection until the meal. According to John the same went for Mary (John 20.2). The empty tomb to her meant that the body had been removed. The empty tomb did not create faith. It is a witness *not to the fact, but to the nature* of the Resurrection and the resurrection body of Jesus.

But is all this talk about a 'resurrection body' conceivable?

Is it conceivable?

Thousands had flocked into Jerusalem for the festival of Pentecost. It was reported that Peter and the other eleven apostles were 'filled with the Holy Spirit and began to speak in other tongues, as the Spirit gave them utterance' (Acts 2.4). The crowds were amazed at what was going on. Peter then preached. The theme of this famous Pentecost 'sermon' was that 'God raised Jesus up, having loosed the pangs of death, because *it was not possible* for him to be held by it' (Acts 2.24). As Henry Drummond once said: 'Maybe it is as normal for a sinless man to rise from the dead, as it is for a sinful man to remain in the grave.'[9]

Perhaps we have to 'expand our minds'. We have to face the fact that the Resurrection will, if it is true, be beyond our experience and to that extent beyond our conception or imagination. But why should we think that it *must* necessarily lie within the limits of our understanding. The unimaginable is not the same as the unbelievable. A century ago no one could imagine how anyone could get to the moon. It would have been incorrect, however, to believe that no one *ever* could get to the moon. As we shall see, the historical truth of the Resurrection is not affected by any difficulty we may have in understanding or explaining it.

The New Testament gives some help to our 'imaginations'. Jesus used the picture of a seed. On one occasion in his ministry he applied this picture to his own death (John 12.24). And Paul takes this picture up in his first letter to the Corinthians. Arguing that Christ's resurrection is a foretaste of the ultimate resurrection of the Christian believer, he says this: 'But some one will ask, "How are the dead raised? With what kind of body do they come?" You foolish man! What you sow does not come to life unless it dies. And what you sow is not the body which is to be, but a bare kernel, perhaps of wheat or of some other grain. But God gives it a body as he has chosen' (1 Cor. 15.35–8).

Paul is implying that the relationship between the human body of our earthly existence and the resurrection body is like the relationship of the seed to the full corn. There is both continuity and radical transformation. We need to use this picture if we have conceptual problems. 'We should have been spared many perplexities,' Bishop Westcott once wrote, 'if we had clung to this figure of the seed.'

This picture gives us identity and difference. There is a direct connection between the bulb and the daffodil; but there is a wonderful difference and transformation. So Paul is in effect saying: 'This is the way, at least, we ought to begin to think about the resurrection of the body.' So we are to believe that resurrection life is richer and deeper than life in the physical body; and the most vital fact is this – it will be *more, not less* than physical life.

There is an importance about the belief that matter, including our bodily matter, is transformed through resurrection and not just wasted. For what sort of a God would it be who created the world out of nothing, *ex nihilo*, to return it into nothing ultimately, *in nihil*? But if ultimately God is going to transform the physical universe 'into something else' beyond our understanding, surely, that makes much better sense. As one theologian puts it: 'it is congruous with the idea of a God who never creates without purpose.'[10] It was Paul himself who said that one day 'the creation itself' will be set free from its bondage to decay and obtain the glorious liberty of the children of God' (Rom. 8.21).

The transfiguration of Jesus, some have argued, may give us another clue to the nature of the resurrection body. Merrill Tenney suggests, for example, that the transfiguration recorded earlier in Jesus' ministry (Mark 9.2–8 and parallels) may be a 'sample of the Resurrection' and this may help us understand his resurrection body.

The transfiguration happened after Jesus had promised his disciples that some of them would not see death until they witnessed the Son of man coming in his kingdom (Matt. 16.28). He then took Peter, James and John up to a high place and was 'transfigured'. This involved a physical transformation. 'His face shone like the sun, and his garments became white as light' (Matt. 17.2). 'Neither the body nor the garments were annihilated and replaced by a different substance, but both were activated into incandescence by the power of deity.'[11]

We will now never fully understand. But *if* the Resurrection happened, nothing is impossible with regard to the body of Jesus. What happened, happened. 'Speaking from the theological point of view,' writes G. E. Ladd, 'if Jesus had actually entered a new realm of existence at his resurrection, there remains no reason to deny the possibility that he could appear to his disciples in completely human form, as the Gospel witness said he did. We are here dealing with a realm of existence unknown to us. If so,

such appearances were condescensions of the risen, exalted Jesus
to the obtuseness and unbelief of his disciples.'[12]

'In Jesus' – the resurrection

Who was it that was most put out by the Apostles' preaching?
We are told that in addition to the priests and the captain of the
temple it was the Sadduccees (Acts 4.1). But why were they so
'up tight'? They would have been used to all sorts of odd ideas
being discussed in the public areas of the temple. Everyday there
would have been groups discussing religious subjects ad nauseam.
Plenty of them talked, no doubt, about 'resurrection'. The Old
Testament had mentioned a hope of resurrection in a few places
(Isa. 25.8; 26.19; Dan. 12.2). There is mention of it in other
Jewish literature. And we know that the Pharisees believed in
the resurrection from the dead. They held the belief that 'there
will be a resurrection of both the just and the unjust' one day
(Acts 24.15).

So what was the problem with the teaching of the Apostles?
What was new about the teaching of this Jewish sect? There
were many such sects. What was special about this 'sect of the
Nazarenes'? It was this. Their leaders taught and said that they
were in a real sense witnesses to the resurrection from the dead
'in Jesus'.

A lot of other people at the time believed that the resurrection
would happen one day. There were many views and stories about
this 'one day', or as it was often called 'the day of the Lord'. No
doubt some found these stories rather fanciful. Others, however,
thought there must be something in them. But here were some
people, not from the lunatic fringes, who said that things had
happened in Jesus. They were saying that the resurrection had
begun. The 'end time' had begun.

There was no abstract theology about this. Nor was this an
imaginative dreaming. Here was an uncomfortable statement that
God had 'at last' set in motion in the resurrection of Jesus the
processes of fulfilling his ultimate purpose for man. If this was
true, it was of enormous significance.

Paul was insistent that this was how the resurrection of Jesus
had to be seen. He describes Jesus' resurrection as a kind of

'first-fruits' (1 Cor. 15.20). This was a picture from farming. The first crop of any harvest was called a 'first-fruit'. It wasn't the harvest itself. Nor was it something totally separate from the harvest. It was a small first part. It was a sign that the harvest had begun.

So the Apostles were *not* teaching that Jesus' resurrection was a 'one off' event – a nice reminder that God was still in control and would do something in the end to sort out all the problems of the world. It was much more than that. They were saying that a 'new age' *had begun*. New possibilities were *now* open to men and women. And because the resurrection of Jesus affected his body, these possibilities mesh in with our present life in the world. There is an 'over-lap' between the present and the 'new age'.

The nuances of this are extremely important. If it is true it means that God is in the process of transforming and recreating this world, not annihilating it. There is a mystery here and we have to keep a balance, for the Apostles taught that the process will only be completed when Christ returns a second time. Then there will be that final renewing, with a 'new heaven and a new earth'. But the beginning of the 'new' overlaps with the present. God is indeed involved in the present; he is not only a God of the future. He is wanting to transform the present (and us); and he will do so, if only we let him.

So we must not see the Resurrection as removed from history. There are some people today who say that the resurrection of Jesus is true, but 'supra-historical'. 'It is not on the plane of history but above it.'

That battle was fought in the first few centuries of the Church's life with the Gnostics. They wanted to separate the activity of God in redemption and salvation from the history of the everyday material world. 'The "spiritual" and the "material" don't mix,' they said. 'No!' said the early Christians, 'Jesus proves that they do.'

This battle continually has to be fought out. For the Bible's message is that God is at work *in history*, not outside it. Maybe we find that embarrassing. It means that God has an interest in our everyday lives – what some people call 'the secular'. He is interested in our private histories and our personal relationships as well as in our national histories and our relationships at the level of society and politics. These are not a matter of indifference to God. One day, so the Apostles taught, we will be held accountable for how we have done. That is the challenge.

Conclusion

The Apostles preached about the 'bodily' resurrection, not the survival of the 'soul' or 'spirit' of Jesus. The tomb was empty, they said. But the Resurrection wasn't a crude 'resuscitation'. It was a transformation to life in the new age that God was beginning 'in Jesus'.

3: The shape of history

A World View

'A new vision of the world – that is what is lacking in most treatments of the death and resurrection of Jesus. Normally we concern ourselves with accounts of a single event isolated from its own horizons and inserted into ours. But to cope with radically different horizons boggles our mind, for we must do justice at once to vast panoramas of thought and to many precise details. It is not surprising that there are so few explorers in this realm, nor that their maps are so sketchy.'[1] So wrote Paul Minnear.

No one can begin to understand what the New Testament is really about or the meaning of the Resurrection without first understanding something of the Old Testament and its 'horizons'. That is why the Old Testament is still the Church's book. To the earliest Christians, the 'scriptures' meant the books of the Old Testament. And it is in the Old Testament that you have a 'vast panorama' against which the events of the life, death and resurrection of Jesus must be understood. Most importantly of all you have in the Old Testament *a total philosophy of history*.

What we think about history involves one of the most crucial decisions of our lives. The basic questions that haunt so many of us – 'Who am I?' 'Where am *I* going?' 'What happens when I die?' 'Is "nature" all there is or is "nature" under the control of something or some*one* else?' 'Is there a moral law that works itself out in public as well as private affairs?' – are all questions related to our beliefs about history.

'Our final interpretation of history is the most sovereign decision we can take,' said Herbert Butterfield, a professor of Modern History at Cambridge; 'and it is clear that every one of us, as standing alone in the universe, has to take it for himself. It is our decision about religion, about our attitude to things, and about the way we will appropriate life. And it is inseparable from our decision about the rôle we are going to play ourselves in that very drama of hsitory.'[2]

No one who reads the Old Testament can doubt that history was of supreme importance to the Jews. But they were not concerned with the minutiae of the events so much. Rather they wanted an overall picture. They were often happy to make 'sweeping' generalisations, so long as they could see the fundamental pattern in the events. They looked back at history because they believed they could see the hand of God *in* the events. Their prophets were 'men of history' too. The prophets' job was to make sure the people correctly understood what God was saying in these situations. And the message that comes through loud and clear from them as you read the Old Testament is this: 'God *blesses* his people when they obey his will in their private and public lives. But when his people ignore his will, they experience *judgment*.' So when they indulge in sexual immorality and degenerate to the level of their Baal-worshipping neighbours, when they neglect the poor and those in need, when social injustice is rife, there is personal and social disintegration. But when there is obedience to God's law there is peace and prosperity.

There were exceptions. Things never always work *exactly* to the book. Job had to learn that. But the exception proves the rule; and the rule was the 'rhythm' of 'blessing' and 'judgment'. That 'rhythm' is one of the basic themes in the Old Testament philosophy of history. The study of that 'rhythm' was indeed a 'prophetic exercise' in itself. It was one of the ways you heard God speaking. It is not surprising to find, then, that the Old Testament historial books, Joshua, Judges, 1 and 2 Samuel and 1 and 2 Kings, were known as 'The Former Prophets' in the Hebrew Bible.

Who is right?

Can this analysis of things be right? Do the facts ever bear it out? In the end that will be a matter of personal judgment and conviction. But it is perfectly possible to use this model or pattern as a way of interpreting events – including modern events. You could use it to look at the state of the Western World in the last half of the twentieth century. You can take, for example, the poor spiritual state of the Western World in the second half of the twentieth century and then put alongside it social and political problems, trends and, even, disasters that have come later. An Old Testament prophet would do so!

If he then suggested a connection of cause and effect, who could be absolutely sure he was wrong? Why should not the spiritual condition of a man or a nation have effect on social and political life?

The Psalmist said: 'Blessed is the man who walks not in the counsel of the wicked . . . but his delight is in the law of the Lord . . . He is like a tree planted by streams of water, that yields its fruit in its season, and its leaf does not wither. In all that he does, he prospers. The wicked are not so, but are like the chaff which the wind drives away' (Ps. 1.1–4).

It is of course perfectly possible to deny this interpretation. Plenty do. There are indeed many other philosophies of history.

The Marxist, for example, will deny the importance of obedience to God as a factor influencing history. He will say that the root problems of society are economic. That is the area where we have to look for a 'causal chain' in history. 'The history of all hitherto existing society is a history of class struggles,' as we hear in the Communist Manifesto.[3] The 'causal chain' that needs to be dealt with is therefore an economic one.

The 'evolutionary optimist' sees things in yet another way. He has no time for the Old Testament or Marx. You certainly don't need a 'revolution'. 'Time' itself will solve all problems. History will bring in a better age by itself. The universe will evolve towards, and finally into, 'utopia'.

And so you can go on. You can have a 'Freudian' analysis of history. Many of us were brought up on school text books that made us think that the fundamental 'causal chain' in history was the 'old boy' network. The playing fields of Eton and the Athenaeum Club in London were what made the world tick.

But, someone may ask, why should we bother to take *one* basic theory alone. Don't all these insights help? Why not see a *range* of pressures or choices as causing the events of history? We can! To some extent everything that happens *before* something else *can* be linked with it. But it is not unreasonable to ask for one 'causal chain' or pattern that is usually significant in human affairs; and therefore one that *always* ought to be responded to, whatever other action may be right and necessary.

The Bible says there is one – a man's or a nation's relationship with God and its consequences.

The shape of history

The meaning we give to history and the 'shape' we give to it are directly related. You will never understand what the Apostles were saying about the Resurrection unless you come to terms with their 'shape of history'. What do we mean by 'shape'?

Broadly speaking there are two basic shapes. There is history seen as an elongated process, a sort of 'line'. On the other hand there is history seen as a cycle of events or a 'circle'.

Anyone who reads the Bible will see that history is pictured in it as 'linear'. There was a beginning and there will be an end. This ambiguous process of the world we experience will not last for ever. Its present condition will one day end. One day Jesus Christ will return a second time. This is what the Bible appears to teach.

It is all very different to some other views of history. Take the Hindu view. In Hindu literature you can read of the cycle of rebirths. Or take Aristotle, the Greek philosopher; he once spoke of the succession of events in history as 'a sort of circle'. Another Greek philosopher said: 'the motion of time joins the end to the beginning and this an infinite number of times.[4] Nietzsche, the nineteenth century German philosopher, believed that the same events would recur at gigantic intervals in an eternal cycle.

But if you have a view of history that is like that and not like the biblical shape, how can you understand that the Resurrection is 'the beginning of the end'? You can't!

So what we find in the New Testament is the Apostles teaching a view of history as *background* to their teaching that Jesus was risen. They did this when they were addressing people without the Biblical or Old Testament view of history. In Athens this happened. Here Paul was addressing people he supposed had a Greek view of history, not unnaturally. So, as we can see from the Acts' summary of Paul's sermon, he preached a 'philosophy of history' along with the rest of what he had to say.

This is how his words are reported: 'God made from one every nation of men to live on the face of the earth, having allotted periods . . . The times of ignorance God overlooked, but now he commands all men everywhere to repent, because he has fixed a day on which he will judge the world in righteousness by a man whom he has appointed, and of this he has given assurance to all men by raising him from the dead' (Acts 17.26, 30–1).

The earliest preaching of the Resurrection was, of course, to men and women who had an Old Testament view of history. But it soon had to be taught to others in the Gentile world. 'When (the gospel of the resurrection of Jesus) was preached to the Greeks a little later by St Paul,' says John Baillie, 'this view of history was preached along with it; and it is only in conjunction with, and in the context of, this view of history that it can ever be intelligently accepted. History as the gospel sees it, begins with God's creation of man in his own image and man's fall from this high estate through pride. This beginning is, however – like all true beginning and ending – itself beyond history: for history is but the on-going of things between the beginning and the end.'[5]

The Kingdom of God

No one can have a true idea of the Biblical view of history without understanding something of 'the kingdom of God'.

At the time of the Resurrection appearances 'the kingdom' was uppermost in the disciples' thoughts. 'Lord, will you at this time restore the kingdom to Israel?' (Acts 1.6), they asked. But what was the background to this idea of 'the kingdom'? What did the 'kingdom of God' mean to first century Jews?

First century Judaism was a mosaic of beliefs. There were various groups believing various things. The 'hope' of the kingdom would have been seen in a number of different ways. Some would have relied heavily on the prophecies of Daniel. They would have looked forward to the coming of a heavenly Son of man who would bring in a kingdom in 'glory' with 'an everlasting dominion' (Dan. 7.14). Others would have looked for a more earthly solution to their problems in the form of a Davidic King. There were ancient prophecies that spoke of a 'root of Jesse' (Jesse was King David's father) who would 'stand as an ensign to the peoples' (Isa. 11.10). 'The Spirit of the Lord would rest upon him' (Isa. 11.2) and he would bring in a golden age of peace and justice; all the nation's enemies would be defeated.

Then there was the community of Qumran by the Dead Sea. They were looking for a holy war in which the wicked would be destroyed as angels gave support to the righteous. Here was a very different sort of 'kingdom' hope. But one thing all were agreed on. And the disciples believed this, too, that first Easter. *The kingdom would be restored to Israel.*

It was against such a background that Jesus had conducted his ministry. The gist of his initial preaching was: 'The time is fulfilled, and the kingdom of God is at hand; repent, and believe in the gospel' (Mark 1.15).

What, however, was the kingdom *he* was bringing in? That was the question the disciples asked. It wasn't a 'political' or 'social' kingdom. He refused the temptation to become a purely social or political leader (Matt. 4.2–10). Indeed, he refused to be made 'king' (John 6.15). In fact he ended not on a throne but on a cross! His kingdom came through suffering for the 'sin of the world' (John 1.29).

This totally shattered the 'kingdom hopes' of the disciples. The evidence is clear: 'They all forsook him and fled' (Mark 14.50). They were not around to help him carry his cross. A stranger had to do that (Luke 23.26); it wasn't someone from the home land of Israel, but from Cyrene in North Africa! Only one disciple seems to have been nearby when Jesus died (John 19.26). And it was a secret disciple, who also was a member of 'the opposition' – the Sanhedrin – that offered to look after the dead body of Jesus, Joseph of Arimathea (John 19.38). Then it wasn't some from the band of chosen disciples that discovered Jesus' body had gone on 'the third day' – the Resurrection morning. It was a few women. The disciples at the time were in hiding (John 20.19). 'The coming of the Kingdom,' says G. E. Ladd, 'was a dead dream, incarcerated in the tomb along with the body of Jesus.'[6] This is how the disciples put it: 'We *had* hoped that he was the one to redeem Israel' (Luke 24.21).

In the light of all this we can understand why Paul said that a 'crucified Messiah' was a 'stumbling block' to the Jews (1 Cor. 1.23). The idea that a Messiah or a 'Christ' (lit. 'an anointed one'), who could inaugurate a kingdom, should die on a cruel cross was unthinkable. But the unthinkable had happened and was about to happen.

In a few weeks after the crucifixion these same disciples who had been so disillusioned were saying just that – 'the Christ' had died. And they said it because something had happened which to them *proved* that Jesus *was* the Messiah or 'the Christ'. And they were saying that they were witnesses to that happening – a truly mighty act of God. For God had raised Jesus from the dead. So the Apostles said to the rest of the Jews: 'Let all the house of Israel therefore know assuredly that God has made him both Lord and Christ, this Jesus whom you crucified' (Acts 2.36).

As they preached this and believed it, they suddenly saw history in a new way. They saw that the death and resurrection of Jesus was all part of 'the definite plan and foreknowledge of God' (Acts 2.23). It was the beginning of the kingdom.

The Last Things

What was that 'definite plan'? We are back to the Bible's total view of history. This is the story, to use the words of the familiar Christmas bidding, of 'the loving purposes of God from the first days of our disobedience unto the glorious redemption brought us by the Holy Child – Jesus.'

The message of the bible is this. God Almighty is a god who acts to save. He manifests himself or 'visits' in the course of world history to make himself and his will clear to men and women. Above all he wants to bring them back to himself, because in their selfishness and stupidity they have rejected him. God was not prepared to abandon mankind, although this was what they deserved.

Instead he called out a people to act for him as a redemptive community in the world. They were to tell others about his love. First there was Abraham and his immediate descendents. Then God renewed his relationship with later generations of his descendents under Moses as they were assuming national identity.

After that there were many ups and downs. Eventually a king was appointed. The second of the kings, David, was 'a man after God's own heart' (1 Sam. 13.14). But his successors in the royal line were not all like that by any means. So then God had to discipline his people by way of national exile in Mesopotamia, miles away from the land of Israel.

In time some of them made their way back home. But sin and selfishness were still present after their return and reestablishment in Judah. There was little missionary zeal. The people of God were not true to their calling – apart from *one*, a man from Nazareth in Galilee. At his baptism at the hands of John these words were 'heard', according to Mark: 'Thou art my beloved Son; with thee I am well pleased' (Mark 1.10). It was *this* one who preached that 'the kingdom of God is at hand'. This was 'the plan'.

But what did he really mean when he also said, 'The time is fulfilled' (Mark 1.15)? What precisely was the fulfilment of 'the plan'?

The Old Testament was always looking forward to a time when God would really 'redeem' his people and the world. The ups and downs of Jewish history meant that something more would have to happen if God's reign or 'kingdom' would come. God would have to act in a decisive way. This great day was called 'the day of the Lord' (Joel 2.31; 3.14). Others called it 'that day' (Amos 9.11; Zeph. 3.11, 16; Zech. 14.9). And the other side of that day lies the 'kingdom'.

This kingdom would include blessings for the Gentiles as well as for the Jews. It was to be a wonderful time. It was to be an era of peace and true happiness. God would be 'king'. It was a panorama of hope.

Now some called this period *after* 'the day of the Lord' *'the latter (or last) days'* (Isa. 2.2–4; Hos. 3.5; Ezek. 38.16). These 'last days' would form the final consummation of history. This is the time when God's purposes would *at last* be fulfilled. This is not the period before the final consummation, a period of the last days of this age. No! 'The latter (or last) days' *are the new age*.

The Old Testament vision was simply of two periods: 'this age' and 'the age to come'. And the division between these two ages was 'the day of the Lord'. And 'the day of the Lord' was the day when the 'fulfilment' would begin.

But note. At the time of Jesus there were plenty of Jewish religious leaders who had come to the following conclusion: ' "this age" is totally evil. The only hope is for a destruction of the old and a replacement by the new. Israel had suffered so much that this would be the only real solution.' It seemed to them as though God had given up.

This was an entirely 'negative' view of the present. We will remember that it has similarities to Gnostic ideas. The authors of the book of Enoch and 4 Ezra from the intertestamental period held this view. God was still 'there'. But he was outside all the conflict and suffering. All that his people could do was to 'grin and bear' it. They must simply wait for an 'apocalypse'.

Fulfilment

We can now see what Jesus meant when he said, 'the time is fulfilled.' In his own person and especially in his death and resurrection something cosmic was happening. At first people could not see it. The disciples at first did not see it. But when the Holy Spirit came at Pentecost it was crystal clear. The Holy Spirit's coming proved that 'the last days' were present in Jesus and his resurrection. 'In the last days it shall be, God declares, that I will pour out my Spirit upon all flesh' (Acts 2.17): so said Peter in his great Pentecost sermon when he was preaching about the Resurrection. No wonder the Apostles were bold! Not only the tomb but history itself had cracked open with the resurrection of Jesus.

And see what this means. The present is not totally bad or without hope. The 'age to come' has begun. The 'last things' have started in history in Jesus and the Resurrection. 'The time is fulfilled, and the kingdom of God is at hand.' True, a 'consummation' is still awaited. Or as Paul would say, quoting an Old Testament Psalm, 'all Christ's enemies are not yet under his feet' (1 Cor. 15.25). Yet Christ is reigning. We are simply waiting for the climax 'when he delivers the kingdom to God the Father' (1 Cor. 15.24). That is still in the future.

The Apostles' teaching, therefore, on the Resurrection was of a breath-taking nature. We can understand why it was so central to them. As you read the narrative of the book of the Acts of the Apostles one thing stands out: the Resurrection message. It is at the heart of the early Christian preaching. The Apostles weren't so much interested in detailing the miracles of Jesus. They weren't so much (early on) interested in his ethical teaching. No! They preached 'in Jesus the resurrection from the dead'. Remember how Judas's place had to be taken by someone who could be a witness to the Resurrection (Acts 1.22). The Apostles saw witnessing to the Resurrection as their main task.

Clearly they talked about other things. And to make sure that Jesus' words and deeds were not forgotten or misrepresented, they were written up. That is how the Gospels came to be. They are an account of 'all that Jesus began (in his early ministry) to do and teach' (Acts 1.1). But the event that gave meaning and relevance to the earthly ministry of Jesus (and so to history, as they believed) was his resurrection from the dead. It was his resurrection that validated his death.

Everything hinges on the Resurrection. Our evaluation of the entire Christian faith, with its distinctive view of history, hinges on this one question, 'Where did Jesus go?' after he was put in Joseph's tomb. Did he go anywhere, or are his bones still somewhere in the soil of Palestine?

Conclusion

To understand the Resurrection we need to understand what the Bible says about 'history' as a whole. Then to understand 'history', we need to understand the resurrection of Jesus.

4: In accordance with the Scriptures

Old Testament pointers

When Paul gave a summary of the gospel in 1 Corinthians 15, he tells us that 'Jesus Christ was raised on the third day *in accordance with the scriptures*' (verse 4).

The early Christians clearly saw the resurrection of Jesus as a fulfilment of the Old Testament hope. It was not so much that the Old Testament had *predicted* the resurrection from the tomb of the Messiah any more than it had predicted his death on a cross. But in retrospect they discovered, as the risen Jesus had shown them (Luke 24.26–7), all sorts of pointers to the Resurrection in the Old Testament.

Before the resurrection of Jesus the disciples were living with preconceptions. They had, no doubt, their own ideas of what was or was not predicted. But the resurrection of Jesus for them turned upside down the whole way they looked at the Old Testament. They now started with Christ rather than the text. They then went back to the text and realised that there was an inner logic in the Old Testament that pointed to Jesus. So as they considered the life, death and resurrection of Jesus and surveyed the whole Old Testament, they saw what Old Testament themes and events Christ fulfilled and how he fulfilled them.

Isaiah 53 obviously pointed to the Crucifixion, with its account of the 'suffering servant' who 'bore the sin of many' (verse 12). Perhaps verse 10 pointed to the Resurrection: 'when he makes himself an offering for sin, he shall see his offspring, he shall prolong his days.' Certainly Paul saw the next chapter of Isaiah, 54, as pointing to the new life and new kingdom established by the resurrection of Christ. In Galatians he applies it to the life of the Church (Gal. 4.27).

Then there were hints of the 'third day' in the Old Testament. We know that in the rabbinical tradition Hosea 6.2 was quoted as a prophecy of the final resurrection: 'After two days he will revive us; on the third day he will raise us up, that we may live before him.' Jonah 1.17 and Leviticus 23.10ff where the offering of firstfruits is to be 'on the morrow after the sabbath', i.e. the Sunday after Passover were other 'third day' texts.

We know, too, that Psalm 16 was seen to be important: 'Therefore my heart is glad, and, my soul rejoices; my body also dwells secure. For thou dost not give me up to Sheol, or let thy godly one see the Pit. Thou dost show me the path of life; in thy presence there is fullness of joy, in thy right hand are pleasures for evermore' (9.11). Peter referred to this Psalm in his Pentecost sermon.

But the Resurrection could also be seen as a fulfilment not only of Old Testament texts but also of Old Testament teaching, in particular its teaching on life after death.

Jewish hopes of life after death

The Old Testament is not vibrant with hope in the way the New Testament is. The resurrection of Jesus was still in the future. Nevertheless there is a clear hope that God will act on behalf of his people and in their favour; but so often it is a hope for the nation rather than the individual. However, nations are made up of individuals and they want to know what lies beyond the grave. There was a fear for the Jew at times not only of being 'cut off from his people' (Lev. 19.8) but also of being cut off from God: 'For in death there is no remembrance of thee; in Sheol who can give thee praise?' (Ps. 6.5) – Sheol being the place of the dead, a place of shadowy existence.

In the earliest period we don't know what was believed about 'coming back to life'. There is little evidence. Perhaps some were aware that the God of Abraham, Isaac and Jacob was not the God of the dead, but of the living, as Jesus said (Mark 12.27); and so 'life' would have victory over 'death'. Quite early on there must have been an awareness that death wasn't *always* the end. We read of Hannah saying: 'The Lord kills and brings to life; he brings down to Sheol and raises up' (1 Sam. 2.6). And the

Israelites believed that the dead had been raised in the time of Elijah and Elisha. Nor was this the mere raising of the spirits of the dead, through forbidden occult practices as in the case of the witch of Endor and the spirit of Samuel (1 Sam. 28). The son of the widow of Zaraphatha and the son of the Shunamite woman were restored to full life (1 Kings 17.17–24; 2 Kings 4.18–37). Then there was the incidence of the corpse thrown into the grave of Elisha. As soon as the dead man touched the bones of Elisha, 'he revived, and stood on his feet' (2 Kings 13.21).

The modern person tends to dismiss these incidents as 'legends'. But as with a number of 'odd' passages in the Bible that is not so easy as it at first seems. Why would they have been created or fabricated for those two prophets alone? There is no tradition of an ability to raise the dead as being part of a prophet's endowment or 'charisma' in the Old Testament. 'In the very full accounts of the activity of the eighth and seventh century prophets,' writes S. H. Hooke, 'nothing of the same kind appears.'[1] It is an interesting fact that the miraculous in the Bible is limited mainly to the ministry of Moses, the ministry of Elijah and Elisha and the ministry of Jesus and his Apostles. Why? If 'writing up miracles' was a way of authenticating great men, why were not David and the kings or other prophets made into miraculous figures?

Be that as it may, the memory of these raisings from the time of Elijah and Elisha may have influenced subsequent belief about resurrection among the Jews. We can't be sure. But, of course, these were only resuscitations. Sheol ultimately still beckoned.

In time a 'fuller hope' becomes more explicit. Certainly you have this in Amos. The prophets generally taught that God was God of the whole universe. He was bigger than the horizons of the land of Palestine. God was interested in the whole world. This was the great message of Amos. Yet perhaps one of his greatest words was that God was sovereign over death as well as over life: 'Though they dig into Sheol, from there shall my hand take them; though they climb up to heaven, from there I will bring them down' (Amos 9.2).

Israel's vision of God was growing. The prophets taught that God was a God who could bring life out of death. True, Ezekiel spoke more of life for a dead nation in his vision of the valley of dry bones (Ezek. 37); so too did Hosea in the verse we have already referred to (Hos. 6.2). But before the Old Testament age closes there is a firm belief, in some quarters at least, that death will not be the end (Job 19.25–6; Ps. 49.15; 73.24; Isa. 26.19). Daniel says this: 'And many of those who sleep in the dust of the earth shall awake, some to everlasting life, and some to shame and everlasting contempt (Dan. 12.2).

It would be wrong, however, to trace too great a linear development of ideas. No doubt various ideas were held among the Jews at the same time. We certainly know this was the case in the intertestamental period. Beliefs then about life after death and the resurrection were varied.

Some, like the Pharisees, believed in resurrection. Others, like the Sadducees, denied it. In one of the books of the Apocrypha in one place it says there is no 'immortality', in another place it says there is (Ecclesiasticus 17.30 and 19.19)! Some believed in a bodily resurrection (2 Maccabees 7.13ff); others, like the Greeks, looked for the survival of the 'soul' (Wisdom 15.8).

But whatever was or was not believed over the whole span of pre-Christian Jewish history, one thing is certain: no one had a belief that the Messiah would rise from the dead as a unique act.

So when the Apostles claimed this is exactly what had happened, they were not claiming a simple fulfilment of Old Testament prediction. Rather they were *filling out* the Old Testament hope. Indeed, the resurrection of Jesus was quite unique and unexpected. 'The central doctrine of the New Testament – that Christ is risen from the dead,' writes Donald Guthrie, 'introduces a unique idea, which had been only imperfectly prepared for in the pre-Christian era. This makes it imperative to explain in an adequate way the rapidity of the spread of the belief in the resurrection of Christ.'[2]

Men of common sense

Exactly *how* the Resurrection is 'in accordance with' the Old Testament scriptures may be a matter for discussion and debate. What is not open to debate is that the Resurrection is 'in accordance with' the *New* Testament scriptures. Both the belief in the Resurrection and the fact or event it rests on are amply docu-

mented for us in the New Testament. But are the documents of
the New Testament reliable?

In some quarters there is an assumption that people in New
Testament times believed anything they were told. 'Today we
have a critical turn of mind,' someone says; 'in ancient times
people believed every report and every rumour they were told.
Someone said a miracle had happened – happened it must have!'

Such an assumption is not borne out by the evidence. The
Jews of the first century certainly did not believe every report
they heard. Nor was the first century AD generally an age of
credulity. Miracles were not automatically believed in. We have
already seen that the Jews according to John did not at first
believe that Jesus had healed a man who was blind from birth.
They had first to interrogate the parents. Indeed for many this
was an age of questioning and scepticism. Thomas the doubting
disciple was a sceptic (John 20.25). The Sadducees, a faction
containing many of the Jewish leaders, refused to believe in 'the
resurrection, angel or spirit' (Acts 23.8).

Outside the borders of Palestine there was also a questioning
spirit. At this time, for example, Roman writers were being very
critical.

Lucretius, a Roman poet, was a thorough-going materialist in
all but name. He wrote his great poem *On the Nature of Things*
to help a friend out of superstitious belief and the fear of pagan
Gods. After describing how Iphigenia had been brutally sacrificed
because of religious prejudice, he penned that famous line:
'*Tantum religio potuit suadere malorum* (religion has been a force
that has brought so much evil).' His main thesis was 'the world
is ultimately only a collection of "atoms", so let's be scientific
and get away from priestcraft and religion.'

Lucretius certainly wouldn't believe just anything he was told.
And don't forget, Roman *ideas* were coming into Palestine in
New Testament times. That in part is why the Jews at the time
of Jesus so hated the Romans.

People in New Testament times, and the Jews in particular,
were capable of examining matters of alleged fact. And they did
this critically. They could weigh evidence and arguments. The
Jews had courts of law as all societies had and have. They could
weigh evidence and decide on whether to accept it or not. They

had a rule that is referred to in the Bible: evidence is to be accepted only if there are at least two or three witnesses (Deut. 19.15; Matt. 18.16; 2 Cor. 13.1).

G. B. Caird, a professor of New Testament at Oxford, reminds us that they used this rule even to settle the calendar: 'on the twenty-ninth of every month the calendar committee of priests sat in their committee room and waited until two witnesses arrived to report that they had seen the first thin crescent of the new moon; if they arrived before six o'clock, then the next day was the first of the new month, and if not, the next day was the thirtieth of the old month. One witness was not enough; there must be at least two, and even then they were closely questioned to make sure that they had seen the crescent moon in the right place and the right way round.'[3]

Perhaps it is significant that we have *four* Gospels and *four* accounts of the resurrection of Jesus. One or two more than was needed – to make absolutely sure!

Legends

The New Testament has a note of common sense about it. This is so clear when we compare what we read there about the resurrection of Jesus with some of the 'legends' that grew up later and are in some of the literature that comes from Gnostic circles.

You can find a number of these texts in the 'New Testament Apocrypha'. They are so bizarre compared with the accounts of the Resurrection in Matthew, Mark, Luke or John.

Here is an account from the so called 'Gospel of Peter.' This is a later Gnostic work that comes from Syria. Serapion the Bishop of Antioch about the year 200 AD once found one or two of his church people reading it, which worried him. This account of the Resurrection is so different from the canonical Gospels. It breathes a different air:

'Early in the morning, when the Sabbath dawned, there came a crowd from Jerusalem and the country round about to see the sepulchre that had been sealed.

Now in the night in which the Lord's day dawned, when the soldiers, two by two in every watch, were keeping guard, there rang out a loud voice in heaven, and they saw the heavens opened and two men come down from there in a great brightness and draw nigh to the sepulchre. That stone which had been laid against the entrance to the sepulchre was opened, and both the young men entered in. When now those soldiers saw this, they awakened the centurion and the elders – for they also were there to assist at the watch. And whilst they were relating what they had seen, they saw again three men come out from the sepulchre, and two of them sustaining the other, and a cross following them, and the heads of the two reaching to heaven, but that of him who was led of them by the hand overpassing the heavens. And they heard a voice out of the heavens crying, "Thou hast preached to them that sleep," and from the cross there was heard the answer, "Yea".'[4]

But in the Four Gospels no one witnessed the 'rising' itself as here. True, there are angelic messengers in the gospel story. However, what they do there is announce a fact: 'He has risen, he is not here' – this was the message of the youthful angel in Mark (16.6). The other differences are so obvious.

The Apostles and those who followed in their footsteps were not naïve. That is why, in the early centuries of the Christian Church, there was the debate about the Canon of the Bible. That is why there was so much discussion as to what books should and should not be 'authorised' and so included in it, and what books were Apocryphal or not to be included. What was wanted were books that were 'apostolic', or that contained the Apostles' teaching. This proves that although there were fertile imaginations at the time – the author of the Gospel of Peter certainly had one – the early Christians could make distinctions. They could distinguish between what looked like the good witness of Apostolic teaching from what looked like fiction. Compared with these apocryphal writings, to use J. B. Phillips phrase, there is a 'Ring of Truth' about the New Testament.

The New Testament evidence

The best way to find out what the New Testament says about the Resurrection is to sit down and read the New Testament! It is amazing how few people do that. It is also amazing what happens when you do. A number of professed sceptics have come to faith through such an exercise. Frank Morrison as a result of coming to faith through studying the New Testament wrote the almost 'classic' *Who moved the Stone?* In his preface he tells us 'it is essentially a confession, the inner story of a man who originally set out to write one kind of book and found himself compelled by the sheer force of circumstances to write another.' He had intended disproving the Resurrection, or at least to 'strip the last phase of Jesus' life of its overgrowth of primitive beliefs.' But, as he tells us, he couldn't because of 'the very stubbornness of the facts themselves.'[5]

But how can we summarise what the Gospels say about the Resurrection? And do the separate accounts agree or disagree?

All four Gospels are *agreed* over the following:

1) Jesus was crucified on the Friday of Passover week.

2) Joseph of Arimathea obtained the body of Jesus from Pilate for burial.

3) The body was wrapped in the traditional linen bandages before being buried.

4) The body was buried in a rock tomb (only John fails to mention the precise nature of the tomb; but he implies that it is a rock tomb by his reference to the 'stone' in chapter 21).

5) Women friends and followers of Jesus visited the tomb on the Sunday morning.

6) They found that the stone closing the tomb had been rolled away, and that the body of Jesus had gone.

7) The risen Jesus appeared to a number of his disciples after Easter.

We can next note some other points of detail over which there is *no disagreement*; but these are not mentioned in all *four* Gospels. For example, Matthew, Mark and Luke mention that the women were onlookers at the burial of Jesus; and Matthew, Luke and John tell us that the tomb was a new one. Matthew reports that a guard was set.

But what about *disagreements* and discrepancies? The most serious is the location of the appearance of the risen Jesus. Matthew, Mark and John record appearances of Jesus to the disciples in Galilee, whereas Luke records only appearances in Jerusalem. (We will leave discussion of this until later.)

The difference in the descriptions of the 'messengers' or 'angels' at the tomb is less important. If there *was* a heavenly 'visitation', how on earth would you describe it? You have to stop in your tracks and think. Luke speaks of 'two men . . . in dazzling apparel' (Luke 24.4); Matthew speaks of one angel (Matt. 28.2–3); Mark refers to a 'young man . . . in a white robe' (Mark 16.5). John mentions 'two angels in white' (John 20.12).

James Martin traces the apparent contradiction here to 'the excitement of the unexpected happenings of that Easter morning and to the inability of the women later to be perfectly clear on points of detail.'[6] Leon Morris says, 'The fact that sometimes we hear of one and sometimes of two need not concern us. As many commentators point out, a spokesman is more prominent than his associates and may be referred to without reference to others . . . Problems there undoubtedly are, but the chief thing these minor differences tell us is that the accounts are independent.'[7]

Of course, the Gospels are not the only New Testament evidence on the Resurrection and the appearances of Jesus. In addition we have Paul's list of resurrection appearances (1 Cor. 15.5–8) and there are references in Acts 1. How does it all fit together?

When we take all the evidence it is true that a complete dovetailing is not easy – but not totally impossible. Michael Green says: 'It is no easier to harmonize all the details of the resurrection accounts than it is to reconcile accounts of the same event in eight different newspapers.'[8] G. R. Beasley-Murray says it is 'extremely difficult, if not impossible, to bring the narratives into a unity'; but he notes that none other than Dorothy Sayers thinks otherwise: 'The divergences appear very great on first sight; and much ink and acrimony have been expended on proving that certain of the stories are not 'original' or 'authentic', but are the accretions grafted upon the first-hand reports by the pious imagination of Christians. Well, it may be so. But the fact remains that *all* of them, without exception, can be made to fall into place in a single orderly and coherent narrative without the smallest contradiction or difficulty, and without any suppression, invention, or manipulation, beyond a trifling effort to *imagine* the natural behaviour of a bunch of startled people running about in the dawn light between Jerusalem and the Garden.'[9]

The nature of 'eye-witness' evidence is not a thing that is always taken sufficiently seriously; this is particular important when the witness is of a traumatic or exciting event. Research has now been done on the nature of 'witnessing' and 'reporting' air disasters. A *predictable* level of discrepancy often occurs; but they are *still actual crashes* that are being witnessed!

In more ordinary events we expect differences and discrepancies in reporting. If you are a school teacher and four boys have been involved in something wrong, you call them up. If they all tell *exactly* the same story, you assume collusion. They have decided to pull a fast one on you. But if they tell it 'as it was' – as they saw what went on – you can work out the truth; you can piece their different accounts together; or at least you can see what is *behind* their accounts. So it is with the four Gospels.

If the Resurrection is true, the disciples must have been in a state of near shock as well as excitement. They weren't journalists with notebooks jotting down details for a good 'exclusive'. Nor were the Gospel writers seeking to put down every thing that happened that first Easter. They clearly were being selective; they had no intention of giving an exhaustive account.

Conclusion

The Jewish people were not naïve. So we have to explain the New Testament reports of the resurrection of Jesus. We can't say the Resurrection is a simple evolution from the Old Testament. The Old Testament only dimly pointed to it. Nor can we dismiss the New Testament reports of it as 'legends'.

5: Is it true?

A common fallacy

Over the last 200 years the Bible has come in for an unprecedented amount of criticism. It is remarkable how well it has stood the test. Emil Brunner tells an interesting story to prove the point: 'Two hundred years ago, scoffing Voltaire, probably the most famous man of his time, prophesied that all would soon be over with the Bible. The house in which this boast was made is to-day one of the offices of a great Bible society. Voltaire's name is almost forgotten; the Bible has had, in the meantime, an incredible career of triumph throughout the world.'[1]

Perhaps one of the greatest causes for distrusting the New Testament records is a common fallacy; and the Bible more than any other book has been subject to this. It is the fallacy that says that if you have explained the origins of something and seen that these are very different to the final product, you have explained *away* the final product.

It is amazing how powerfully destructive a knowledge of origins can be. But, of course, to know the origin of something is irrelevant often as far as its present value, truth or effectiveness is concerned. A man may be born in a log cabin. But if he ends up in the White House as President of the United States of America, he is the President no matter what his origins. Modern astronomy may have evolved from astrological guesswork in ancient Babylon. But if men can travel to the moon and back today, it is clearly more than guesswork now. So it is with the Bible.

The four Gospels may well be the result of godly men in the mid-first century AD collecting earlier written sources as 'Source Criticism' has suggested. Or the Gospels may have resulted in part from regularly told short stories from the life of Jesus as 'Form-Criticism' has suggested. And most probably the Gospel writers put their material together, from whatever source, to emphasise a particular truth about God's revelation of himself in Jesus Christ, as 'Redaction-Criticism' has suggested. But by itself all this tells us nothing about whether what we have got as the final product is true or false, accurate or inaccurate. Something in the Gospel narrative may be said by the scholars to come 'from "Q" (a collection of Jesus' teachings) or from "M" (Matthew's special source)' or to come 'in the "Form of a miracle-story" '. But by itself that tells us nothing as to whether *what* comes like that is true or false. The mere fact that the report of a miracle may be given in a stylised way tells us little. The question 'Was there a miracle there in the first place?' is a different question from 'How has the report of the alleged miracle come down to us?'

Tradition

The gospel of the resurrection of Jesus Christ was originally passed on by word of mouth. The Resurrection happened (or something happened). The Apostles then spoke about it and 'preached' it and they spoke about Jesus. Maybe some of them had taken down notes earlier of specific teachings of Jesus; but there is no record of these in the Acts of the Apostles. All we hear about is 'preaching'. All we can be certain of is an oral tradition. But such an oral tradition would have been nothing new.

In the Old Testament there must have been an 'Oral Tradition'. It is not unreasonable to think of the stories of the patriarchs and the judges as being handed down by word of mouth and repeated at the various sanctuaries; these would have been associated with the various Old Testament heroes. It has been suggested that Abraham may have been associated with Shechem and Hebron, Isaac with Beersheba, Jacob with Bethel and Shechem and Gideon with Ophrah. In addition stories would have been handed down within the various tribes and clans. But of course often the 'tradition', or the 'handing down', would have related to large spans of time.

Take the sojourn in Egypt and the Exodus; or take the settlement in Canaan, or the period of the Monarchy or the period when successively the Assyrians, the Babylonians and the Persians were the superpowers. These were centuries long. The oral tradition in those days covered hundreds of years. Nor is there anything odd about this. You get it in other ancient cultures. And from what we know of some of these there is evidence of a very *tight* oral tradition. In the period of the passing on of material by word of mouth, before it is eventually written down, it is handed on in relatively careful ways. You can think for example of the Homeric poems, *the Iliad* and *the Odyssey*; here the verse form acts as a control. This can be paralleled at various stages of European literature.

Inevitably in the transmission of Old Testament material before it was written down there would have been stylisation. That is to say the way you tell one story is influenced by the way you tell a different story. Details may get lost. But there is *no evidence that you can invent 'ad lib'*.

But – and it is a very big but – the New Testament is totally different to all of this. As has been well pointed out 'the period of the New Testament covers fewer decades than the Old Testament covers centuries.'[2]

Eventually, after the initial preaching, the New Testament Gospels or the sources behind them came to be written down. What had been repeated orally, by word of mouth, was now in a manuscript, a hand-written document, and to that extent fixed.

But prior to that 'fixing' had the 'tradition' been radically modified? That is the big question. Had the oral tradition grown? Of course oral tradition can grow.

But the check on the growth of any tradition is the fact of other people being around who know differently. They can let it be known that certain things are fiction. This means that the presence at large of 'eyewitnesses' of any alleged event that has now become a 'tradition' is of first rate importance.

This is highly relevant for our evaluation of the New Testament. Even at the end of the first century AD a few eyewitnesses of the ministry of Jesus and of the events surrounding his death and resurrection were still alive. There were many more who had known and spoken with eyewitnesses. They heard their reports of what they had seen and heard. 'Some people seem to imagine that, after the initial telling of the story (of the life, death and resurrection of Jesus) every eyewitness immediately and for ever withdrew from the whole affair. The fact is that right up to the beginning of the stage of writing and well on into it, there were in the church surviving eyewitnesses whose oversight of the tradition must have been sufficient to ensure substantial accuracy in its transmission.'[3]

Memory span

It is clear that there were written accounts of the gospel events *earlier* than the four Gospels as we have them (Luke 1.1). And we have Paul's statement on the resurrection appearances in the first epistle to the Corinthians. This was made ten or fifteen years earlier than the usual dating of Mark's Gospel. There were thus accounts of the Resurrection nearer to the events than the Gospels themselves. But leaving all that aside and just thinking about the finished product of Mark's Gospel, we need to remember that even this was published only thirty-five years or so after the Resurrection.

C. H. Dodd, the New Testament scholar, once said that in his younger days he felt this gap of thirty-five years to be a 'very serious matter.'[4] Later in life he came to see that such a period was not so long after all. In a Radio broadcast in 1949 he said that he and his contemporaries had a very vivid memory of the events of the summer of 1914 just prior to the outbreak of the first World War. He went on: 'When Mark was writing there must have been many people who were in their prime under Pontius Pilate, and they must have remembered the stirring and tragic events of that time at least as vividly as we remember 1914. If anyone had tried to put over an entirely imaginary or fictitious account of them, there would have been middle-aged or elderly people who would have said (as you or I might say) "You are wasting your breath: I remember it as if it were yesterday!" '

As I write this on my typewriter, I hear over the Radio that today is the thirtieth anniversary of the death of King George VI. On that day there was a new Queen of the United Kingdom. I can remember quite vividly standing in my school hall and being told by the headmaster of the King's death. I can remember many events from that period; it was when I was at the top end of the Junior School. I could not necessarily give you an accurate chronological *sequence* of all the events; but I could recount a lot of them as isolated events. Most important of all if someone came along and said that something major had happened at the school when it hadn't, or he totally misrepresented what had happened, I would be able to say he was speaking nonsense.

And, of course, where there is a great deal of teaching by word of mouth memory becomes more important. It appears that the Jewish Rabbis employed memorising techniques in their transmission of teaching.[5] Clearly Jesus was different to the other religious teachers of his day; we cannot assume that he copied their teaching techniques anymore than he copied their teaching. But in a culture where memory was important, a cavalier approach to the passing on of facts and information is not to be expected. In fact in such a culture memory is often developed to a high degree; and people have better memories than many of us have in our instant 'electronic recall' world! This apparently is true in parts of India where the training of the verbal memory is regarded as being very important.[6]

Prophets and private revelations

But what about the influence of 'Christian prophets' in developing and creating tradition. Some might say: 'People will ignore memory when a "prophet" is around and be afraid to contradict when a man says, "I, the Lord speak to you." Perhaps Christian prophets made up edifying stories.' The evidence for this is non existent. In any case prophets are always 'the odd man out'. As far as the majority is concerned they find them an embarrassment. That prophets should have been responsible for the creation of fictions about the life, death and resurrection of Jesus is unthinkable. 'The role of prophets in the formation of the tradition,' says F. F. Bruce, 'has been greatly exaggerated. We have simply no concrete evidence to indicate that prophets in church meetings uttered words in the name of the exalted Lord which were preserved in the tradition as sayings of Jesus "in the days of his flesh." From the few details of prophetic utterances that have been recorded in the New Testament, they seem to have been pedestrian in character, relating to *ad hoc* situations.'[7]

To assume that prophets were responsible for words and deeds ascribed to Jesus in the four Gospels is hardly worth refuting. To assume that prophets could have given rise to the Resurrection is, of course, even more ridiculous.

Another check on the development of fictitious ideas and stories was the fact that the gospel was not private. This is very significant. It was the Gnostic sects that believed in 'secret' revelations; it is not surprising that bizarre and obviously fictional stories about the life, death and resurrection of Jesus emerged from them. But the Church under the Apostles believed that the gospel belonged to the church as a whole. There was something corporate about it. It was an 'open secret'.

So there was a concern for the 'unity' of the tradition. People wanted to check up on the facts. Paul himself wanted to consult with the Christians in Jerusalem. In one sense he was totally independent of Jerusalem and doing a quite separate work in his Gentile mission. But he decided early on to go up to Jerusalem to check things out. He decided to put before the leaders there 'the gospel which I preach among the Gentiles, lest somehow I should be running or had run in vain' (Gal. 2.2). Paul clearly believed that he had received his commission and his gospel directly from the exalted Christ. He had not received it from the Jerusalem leaders (Gal. 1.1). But he 'checked it out' with them.

There is no evidence for individual Christians in the early Apostolic Church having 'private' visions and on that basis generating 'stories'.

John's Gospel

The Gospels are four different accounts of the life, death and resurrection of Jesus Christ. They are quite unique in the history of literature; they are not biographies in the modern sense. A disproportionate amount of them is given over to the last week of Jesus' life. John says of what he has written in his Gospel, especially the 'signs' – and the greatest sign is the Resurrection – that he has been selective. He has only written a fraction of what he could (John 21.25). He says: 'These are written that you may believe that Jesus is the Christ, the Son of God, and that believing you may have life in his name' (John 20.31). John clearly had a theological purpose. But he is not for the moment suggesting he is fabricating 'signs'. He says he makes his theological points by *selection* from actual incidents and events – that is what he thought he was doing; there is not the slightest hint he was making his theological points by the *creation* of imagined incidents and events. But can we trust John?

John's Gospel has had a recent 'rehabilitation'. For many years it was said that John's Gospel was written late. It was said that the writer, whoever he was (and according to this view he certainly had nothing to do with the Apostle John of the twelve), just took Matthew, Mark and Luke and rewrote them! He rewrote the facts even! This was the reason, it was said, why John seems so different from the other three synoptic gospels (synoptic means literally 'seeing together'). But the argument went on like this: if John could freely rewrite the other existing Gospels, why shouldn't those other three have done just the same thing with their sources? Why not indeed?

Then C. H. Dodd gave the Sarum Lectures for 1954–55. These were published as *Historical Tradition in the Fourth Gospel*. He proved overwhelmingly that John was not dependent on the other Gospels for his sources. He did not rewrite them therefore. He couldn't have done. Rather, Dodd showed, in John's Gospel we have an independent tradition of material from Southern Palestine. We can't dismiss what John says about the Resurrection.

So now when C. H. Dodd comes to look at the narratives in John about the Resurrection and in particular Peter and John's visit to the tomb, he sees evidence of eyewitness rather than fabrication. He sees this in the account of the two Apostles' visit to the tomb. When they got there, they 'saw the linen cloths lying, and the napkin, which had been on his head, not lying with the linen cloths but rolled up in a place by itself' (John 20.6–7).

The body of Jesus had been wrapped in long strips of cloth and spices had been put in between. The 'napkin' was a separate piece of linen wrapped over the head and under the chin to keep the jaw in place. What John's Gospel says is that when John saw these 'cloths' he believed. He believed, that is to say, not when he saw the empty tomb, but when he saw the 'napkin' still separate from the rest of the linen wrappings that had been round the trunk and legs; it seemed as though the body had passed through the linen cloths. This was no resuscitation. It was a resurrection! The body had not revived, it had disappeared. 'The story,' says Dodd, 'is told with dramatic realism of which this writer is master. It looks something as near first-hand evidence as we could hope to get. Perhaps it is, and if so, it becomes the sheet anchor of belief in a "bodily resurrection".'[8]

Again it was Dorothy Sayers who was quite convinced of the 'eyewitness' nature of John's Gospel. Looking at the Gospel as a novelist herself and so from the viewpoint of someone used to 'creating' or 'fabricating stories', she says this: 'It must be remembered that, of the four Evangelists, St John's is the only one that claims to be the direct report of an eyewitness. And to anyone accustomed to the imaginative handling of documents, the internal evidence bears out the claim.'[9]

Luke's Gospel

But John is not the only Gospel writer who tells us what he is aiming to do as he selects his material. Luke also tells us of his aims. 'In as much as many have undertaken to compile a narrative of the things which have been accomplished among us, just as they were delivered to us by those who from the beginning were eyewitnesses and ministers of the word, it seemed good to me also, having followed all things closely for some time past, to write an orderly account' (Luke 1.1–3).

Despite attempts to discredit Luke over the years, it is quite remarkable how he has withstood the test. Indeed what is noticeable is how modern experts who approach the New Testament from the view point of secular ancient history find Luke convincing. Those used to evaluating ancient documents and sources from the classical world of Greece and Rome say Luke is a good historian. A. N. Sherwin-White, a Roman Historian, is amazed at the scepticism of some New Testament critics. Having examined the New Testament, especially Luke and Acts, from the view point of Roman law and culture he finds it remarkably reliable.[10]

One of the reasons why Luke has been 'attacked' is because he has an interest in the miraculous. This is undeniable.

'Sober criticism,' writes G. B. Caird, 'cannot get behind the gospel record to a plain, commonplace tale, devoid of the miraculous and the supernatural. The early Christians believed that, in Christ, God had been at work in new and astonishing ways and they had the evidence of their own eyes to support their faith. Luke cannot justly be accused of exaggerating the miraculous element in his narrative. He omits Mark's most difficult miracle, the story of the barren fig tree. It is true that he also goes one step beyond Mark in recording a cure performed at a distance by word of command, but this story, the healing of the centurion's servant, was taken from Q, his most trustworthy source. He has sometimes been taken to task for emphasising the physical nature of the Resurrection since it is in his Gospel alone that the risen Jesus eats and drinks with his disciples. But here too he is simply reproducing with fidelity the sources on which he was relying. For in Acts 10.37–43 he puts into the mouth of Peter an almost credal utterance which is clearly derived from an Aramaic source and which presents the same picture of the Resurrection as we find in the Gospel.'[11]

How accurate is accurate?

But how accurate are the four Gospels? For example, did Jesus ever actually say, 'I am the Resurrection and the life' as is reported in John's Gospel? Professor R. P. C. Hanson, a bishop, who also was a professor of Theology, once suggested it was an incredible thing to believe that Jesus actually said such words.[12] But is there not confusion here?

Of course, few if any would believe that Jesus actually uttered the *syllables* 'I am the Resurrection and the life.' Most know that Jesus spoke neither in English nor always in the Greek of John's Gospel but often in Aramaic. But what many, including experts, would want to say is that Jesus said something somewhere in Palestine which through the agency of tradition and translation has come down to us in English as 'I am the Resurrection and the life.' And we will not be misled if we take this as the gist of what he taught.

We need to understand the nature of New Testament reporting. It followed its own conventions. The Gospel writers saw no problem in 'paraphrasing' or giving the 'gist' of someone's speech and then putting it as direct speech. They would have put this between inverted commas if they'd been invented! R. T. France of the London Bible College comments: 'The use of inverted commas in (our) translations of the Gospels may lead us to expect, on the basis of our own conventions in reporting speech, a degree of verbatim accuracy which the writer did not intend. So many of the sayings which the Gospels introduce with "Jesus said" may in fact be paraphrases. But that does not mean they are inventions.'[13] Someone once said the Evangelists are intending 'to report accurately the substance of Jesus' teaching in meaningful terms to their readers, not to record his precise words in every instance.'

You may say, 'This is all very well with regard to Jesus' own *statements* about the Resurrection and any other element of his *teaching*. But what about the reporting of *events*. Here we want real accuracy. Events are too important.'

But how accurate is accurate when reporting an event? There is just no answer. There is no answer to the question, 'How precise must a description of something be for it to be accurate?' Let me explain.

'Accuracy' is tied in very much with the context of a given report. What determines whether something is 'accurate' or not is not only the description or report itself, but where and when it was given.

The point is this: what is accurate or precise *enough* for some purposes will be inaccurate or imprecise for others. Here is an example.

Imagine being asked the question, 'Is it accurate to say that William the Conqueror landed at Hastings?' What do you say? The proper answer is, 'It all depends.' It all depends on where and when that question is being asked.

It could be asked of a group of ordinary people on some popular TV quiz game. The multiple choice question before the contestants is 'Where did William the Conqueror land – Newcastle, Hull, Hastings or Portsmouth?' The correct answer *in this context* is 'Hastings'. In this context that would be the 'accurate' answer; to say 'Newcastle' would be inaccurate.

But the same question could be asked in a very different context. It could be asked at some South Coast local History Society meeting. The members are interested in an answer that details which part of the Hastings area. The correct answer then would be Pevensey. That is fair enough. But it is not fair then to say, *because of this possibility*, that the person who pressed the 'buzzer' for Hastings in the TV game is wrong and inaccurate. Indeed that would be most misleading! It would be very wrong to have this more detailed context in mind if you were on the TV panel game. You wouldn't get any points! The 'level of generality' has been suggested by the options – Newcastle, Hull, Hastings or Portsmouth. In *that* context to refuse to admit that William landed at Hastings (or near enough to Hastings) is simply not playing the right 'language game', let alone the TV game! It is, therefore, not communicating. If you denied he landed at Hastings, some people would think you were implying he had landed at Hull or one of the other ports.

Now this sort of thing happens in the Bible regularly when people say 'it is not true' or 'it is inaccurate.' 'Accuracy' is a variable; but, as a caution, that doesn't mean to say that anything goes. Some things are just 'inaccurate' and some things are certainly 'not true'. It is untrue and not accurate in *any* context to say that William the Conqueror landed at Newcastle.

When you try to assess the four Gospels the important thing is to realise what 'level of generality' is being presupposed. From what has already been said we can have some idea. Within that context the conviction of Christians down the centuries are that the records are accurate enough. That is why they say the New Testament is true.

Conclusion

The origins of the Gospels may be complicated, but that doesn't entitle us to dismiss their evidence. There were surviving eyewitnesses and other factors to prevent gross exaggeration in reporting or pious additions. There is every reason for saying we are dealing, in the Gospels, with 'accurate' records.

6: 'The one disconcerting fact'

Hard thinking

In 1747 a book was published on the Resurrection. It was written because the author had read two defences of the biblical accounts of the resurrection of Jesus and found them inadequate. He realised that those who read his book would not be 'those who seek in books for nothing more solid than entertainment.' He realised that it was hard work getting to grips with the issues of the Resurrection. But his main contention was that so many people had rejected or neglected the Resurrection without ever trying to come to grips with the issues.

His name was Gilbert West. At that time Christianity was scorned by many. 'I am not ignorant,' he tells us, 'how little reputation is to be gained by writing on the side of Christianity, which by many people is regarded as a superstitious fable, not worth the thoughts of a wise man.'[1]

We tend to think that previous generations were made up of believers; scepticism, we feel, is something modern. That is obviously not true. In the eighteenth century, as today, there were many who never considered the evidence. So Gilbert West had printed on his title page a verse from the Old Testament Apocrypha: 'Blame not before thou hast examined the truth; understand first and then rebuke' (Ecclesiasticus 2.7).

In his introduction he spelt this out: 'Whoever hath either neglected, or doth refuse to make this examination, can have no right to pass his judgment upon Christianity, and should methinks for the same reason be somewhat cautious of censuring those, who acknowledge it to be of divine institution.' We must therefore *think* about some of the issues further. And we need to be rigorous in our thinking.

There is what has been called 'a strangely perverse attitude' among many people.[2] They too readily accept what has been called 'the latest irresponsible speculation by the journalistic charlatans,' and they treat in a cavalier fashion the documents and the evidence of the New Testament.

The empty tomb

We shall go over some of the issues. The empty tomb has been 'attacked' in two ways.

Some say that the early Christians themselves did not really believe in an empty tomb. All the stories about the empty tomb have been concocted late in the day and then inserted by the Gospel writers into their accounts. Paul, it is said, didn't believe in the empty tomb. He thought the bones of Jesus were still in the grave. The idea of a 'bodily' Resurrection was a late addition, superimposed on an earlier 'spiritual' resurrection tradition.

Others say the tomb was empty, but not because of the Resurrection, but because Joseph of Arimathea had removed the body; or Jesus had not really died – he had only swooned; or the women had gone to the wrong tomb; or even the disciples had stolen the body. This last was one of the first 'alternative' hypotheses. It is mentioned in the New Testament (Matt. 28.13). Another early 'alternative' was, according to Tertullian, 'the theory that the gardener of the tomb removed the body of Jesus and placed it elsewhere to protect his lettuces from the spectators!'[3]

What can be said in reply to these suggestions? First, why on earth would the early Christians have wanted to create an 'empty tomb' tradition? Had they wanted to do that, they would, surely, have made it fit in better with Jewish expectations of 'resurrection'. These were more in the way of 'resuscitation' as we have seen.

However, if Jesus' resurrection was 'spiritual' only, why did they not say so? When the disciples saw the risen Jesus, we are told, they thought he was a 'spirit' (Luke 24.37). If he had only been that, why deny it? Such a 'positive' apparition of a 'spiritual Jesus' could have made them revise their ideas about the 'spiritual world'. Jesus had made them revise a number of cherished ideas during his earthly ministry. Why should he not now be making them revise their ideas about this? If Jesus was now a spirit, why not say so?

The fact of the matter as we have seen it is that the earliest strata of the Gospel tradition makes it clear that the risen Jesus was believed to have flesh and bones!

It is said that the early Christians created these empty tomb stories to counter Gnostic and docetic tendencies: the Gnostics and Docetics said that matter was bad and Jesus was 'separate' from matter.

But why counter these views? They come easily enough to many people. There would be no reason for countering them unless there was something that led the early Christians to say that they were wrong! The belief that Jesus had a resurrection *body* would be one of the key factors in convincing the early Christians that matter was good. It was not bad.

But did Paul believe that the bones of Jesus were still in the tomb? The argument is that in the first epistle to the Corinthians chapter fifteen he says only that 'Christ died . . . that he was buried, that he was raised' (verses 3–4). He doesn't explicitly mention Jesus leaving the tomb.

However that is pure pedantry. It is clear that 'what was raised on the third day' was 'that which died *and* was buried' – the body of Jesus. 'The natural implication would be that the resurrection was (so speak) the reversal of the entombment.'[4] True it was a 'glorified' body. But Paul is quite clear that such a body came about not by leaving the old body to rot and having a new body, but by a 'change' of the old body. When he refers to the believer at the last day, he says this: 'We shall not all sleep (i.e. some, not all, will go to their graves), but we shall all (the dead and the living) *be changed*' (1 Cor. 15.51). As he believes that the resurrection of Jesus was the 'firstfruits' of the resurrection of every believer, we must assume he saw the resurrection of the believer and the resurrection of Jesus as similar. We must assume therefore he believed that Jesus body *changed*.

Further, if the tomb was not empty, why didn't someone produce the body? This point has been made so many times but has never yet been satisfactorily answered. Professor D. M. Mackinnon speaks of 'the inability of the opponents of the early

Christian preaching to silence the message of the Resurrection once for all by producing Christ's remains.'[5]

One other point – why, oh why, if the empty tomb was being devised for 'apolegetic' purposes late in the day were the majority of witnesses to the tomb said to be women? Why weren't the witnesses of the empty tomb made to be men and Apostles at that? In Jewish law the witness of women was suspect.

You cannot escape the empty tomb. Geza Vermes, a Jewish biblical scholar, wrote an article in the *Observer Colour Supplement* on 'The Mystery Tomb'. He is not friendly to the Christian account of things, but he has to admit: 'the one disconcerting fact; namely that the women who set out to pay their last respects to Jesus found not a body but an empty tomb.'[6] C. H. Dodd again sums it up well: 'When they (the early Christians) said "He rose from the dead", they took it for granted that his body was no longer in the tomb: if the tomb had been visited it would have been found empty. The Gospels supplement this by saying, it *was* visited, and it *was* found empty.'[7]

The tomb was empty, but . . .

It needs to be admitted that the early Christians did not base their belief in the Resurrection on the empty tomb. In fact they often seemed to have played it down. It was not the main plank of their early preaching, although it is implied by it.

Negative evidence is of doubtful value; and the empty tomb is negative evidence. So it is not surprising to read in Mark that the women who discovered the tomb to be empty 'said nothing to anyone' (16.8). Luke tells us that the other disciples treated the story of the empty tomb as 'an idle tale' (24.11).

The main reason why the disciples believed that Jesus had risen was that they *saw* him alive after his death. The empty tomb enabled them to understand a little of what actually they had seen. They hadn't just seen 'visions'.

But what serious alternative explanation of the empty tomb can you give? And remember all four Gospels admit to it. Remember, too, there are 'semiticisms' that show the accounts come from early Palestinian sources.[8] How can you then account for the 'emptiness' other than by the Resurrection?

200 years ago Venturini tried to say that Jesus had never really died. The wounds of the Crucifixion merely made him 'swoon'. By mistake he was taken down from the cross too early before he had really expired.

This view ignored the evidence of John's Gospel that says measures were taken to make sure death had occurred. To continue to hold such a view today ignores the powerful criticism of D. F. Strauss (1808–74), a theologian who himself denied most of Christianity! But he showed the impossibility of someone who had gone through the horrors of crucifixion giving rise to 'resurrection' faith. A poor, dehydrated creature, racked with pain and requiring enormous care and attention to help survive could not, he argued, have generated such a belief.[9]

But nothing daunted, Hugh Schonfield tried a modern version of this in *the Passover Plot*. He there tries to say that Jesus *intended* to fake death. He wanted a mock 'sacrificial' death. He planned that collaborators should help him back to life. Unfortunately he hadn't banked on the 'spear-thrust', so everything misfired. He may have revived for a short time, during which period an unknown person took messages from the dying Jesus to the disciples. This person was mistaken for Jesus hence the belief in the Resurrection!

All that can be said for this view is that it has made Dr Schonfield's book a 'million-copy bestseller'! That is on the cover of my edition.[10] It is sheer fantasy. As J. N. D. Anderson points out, there is no suggestion 'as to why the unknown messenger was mistaken for Jesus himself, why the conspirators never told the apostles what really happened, or what, indeed, would have been the outcome of this fantastic plot if it had succeeded.'[11] Frank Morrison called the 'swoon-type' theories 'really little more than an historical curiosity'.[12] But Hugh Schonfield shows that it has, for one reason or another, a certain persistence. The theory owes it strength to the evidence that the tomb *was* empty.

Earlier than Venturini, Hermann Reimarus put forward an even more bizarre theory. He said that the disciples had done quite well out of Jesus ministry. They had been able to live off it as a sort of 'hippy band'. 'What a pity,' they said, 'if we have to give all this up' – or words to that effect. They did not fancy the more routine life of a fisherman or tradesman. So they stole the body of Jesus, hid it and told everyone that one day he would return! This enabled them to carry on as before. Beasley-Murray has said it all: 'Suggestions of this kind are nothing less than contemptible.'[13] People will lie to make money; but they will not lie to die. We are asked to believe the disciples were prepared to be martyred for this lie!

But could someone else have stolen the body? Why? And how was the body concealed when all Jerusalem was talking about the Resurrection and the Jewish leaders wanted the body. The evidence of Judas' dealings with the chief priests shows that there was money to be made from cooperating with them (Luke 22.5).

Kirsopp Lake put forward another idea. The women went to the wrong tomb. They found a young man who most helpfully said: 'he is not here (in this tomb); see the place where they laid him.' Professor Lake adds, he 'probably pointed to the next tomb. But the women were frightened at the detection of their errand and fled.'[14] Some days later they assumed, in the light of what the Apostles told them, that they had been to the right tomb.

But Kirsopp Lake doctors or ignores the evidence. He bases what he says on Mark alone and then misses out crucial words. For Mark says the 'young man . . . in a white robe' said to the women: 'you seek Jesus of Nazareth, who was crucified. *He has risen*, he is not here; see the place where they laid him' (Mark 16.6). The other Gospels say the Apostles went to check on the tomb! Again, why didn't the Jewish authorities go themselves and explore and find the right tomb? They could have produced the body to silence things once and for all.

That they didn't, argues against the Jewish authorities themselves ever moving the body. Yet did Joseph of Arimathea do so? If he did and if he was a secret disciple, as the New Testament says (John 19.38), why didn't he tell the other disciples? If he was a Jewish plant, why didn't he tell the Jewish authorities?

It is important to remember that the only argument that the Jewish authorities at the time came up with was that the disciples had stolen the body. At that time they could not have realised that this would be disproved by the disciples' willingness to die for their risen Lord. At the time they must have believed this was the best they could try. Any other suggestions they knew

held no water. In time the theory that the disciples had stolen the
body was seen for what it was, a tissue of lies (Matt. 28.12–13).

The appearances

The resurrection faith was based more on the appearances of
the risen Lord than on the empty tomb. But what were these
appearances?

The earliest record of the appearances is in Paul's first letter
to the Corinthians chapter fifteen. This takes us back a very long
way behind the Gospels. Paul was writing about 25 years after
the death of Jesus, but this account was passed on to him many
years before that. It looks as though it was passed on to him at
the beginning of his Christian experience. He considers this to
be a matter 'of the first importance'. It therefore relates to the
heart of the Christian faith.

'For I delivered to you as of first importance, what I also
received, that Christ died for our sins in accordance with the
scriptures, that he was buried, that he was raised on the third
day in accordance with the scriptures, and that he appeared to
Cephas, then to the twelve. Then he appeared to more than five
hundred brethren at one time, most of whom are still alive,
though some have fallen asleep. Then he appeared to James, then
to all the Apostles. Last of all, as to one untimely born, he
appeared also to me' (1 Cor. 15.3–8).

Paul is appealing to common knowledge. People can go and
ask any of the people he has mentioned. There was Peter
(Cephas), the leader in the immediate period after the Crucifixion
and Resurrection. There was James, Jesus' brother. He became
the leader of the Jerusalem Church when Peter moved out and
about. Paul knew them both well and had spent a fortnight with
Peter just a few years after the death and resurrection of Jesus.
This was on his visit to Jerusalem we have already referred to.
This is evidence very close to the events.

Something had happened. What had happened was not the
occurrence of a 'religious consciousness'. No! People said they
had *seen* Jesus. And it was a particular series of 'seeings'. They
were quite unique. They were confined to a limited period.
Everyone knew that at a certain point these events had come to

an end. That is why Paul was so insistent that when he 'saw the Lord' it was quite unexpected and abnormal, 'an appendix to a series already closed.'[15]

One of the things that can be said with conviction about the Resurrection appearances recorded at the end of the Gospels is that they are so different from one another. But they all left those who had seen the risen Jesus with an unshakeable conviction: they had not seen a ghost or a spirit but at least a real person

Some of the appearances are recounted in detail. We read of Mary in the garden, thinking she is seeing the gardener (John 20.15). We read of Jesus suddenly appearing to the disciples behind locked doors (John 20.19). We read of two unknown disciples walking along the road near Jerusalem with a stranger who turns out to be Jesus (Luke 24.13–31). Then he is by the lakeside in Galilee (John 21.1). These are familiar to many people. But we have no details of the appearance to James or to the 'more than five hundred'.

How can we attempt to describe what happened? We can't. Nor could the Gospel writers with any precision. They could only record what the disciples saw and touched (or tried to touch). 'In describing occurrences which, *ex hypothesi*, lay on the extreme edge of normal human experience, or beyond it, the writers are hardly to be pinned down to matter-of-fact precision in detail.'[16]

Explanation

'This then is where you are arguing in the dark,' someone says. 'We can therefore never say anything useful about what happened.'

A lot of play is made by some of the fact that if these events happened, they must have been 'beyond history'; so the historian might as well give up talking about them. They are matters for 'faith' alone, not historical argument. The historian doesn't have the tools for dealing with what is 'beyond history'. He has nothing to compare this sort of thing with. 'It is without analogy,' as they would say. It is quite unique. How can you begin to talk about something that is so unique?

That is a fair question. But you don't have to be reduced to silence when something strange comes along. True, we very often *do* explain things by 'analogy'. We say that something is similar to something else, but it differs in this or that respect. We 'class' it along with something else of the same 'class' of things, and then we define its 'differences'. We explain what a Bible is, for example, by saying it is a 'religious book' – its 'class'; we then mark it off from other religious books by saying it is the *'Christian religious book'* – its 'differentia', as the philosophers would say.

But you can't do that with something that is unique. It has no 'analogy'; there is nothing else really like it. Like the Resurrection, there is nothing else in history to put it alongside, or a 'class' of similar things to put it in. So you can't begin to mark it off and distinguish it from other similar events, which, it is said, is the essence of any sort of explanation.

You are not then, however, reduced to silence over explaining the Resurrection (or for that matter any other unique item). For not all explanation is undertaken in the way we have just outlined.

Take a 'trick' in a game of cards.[17] How do you explain that. It is quite unique. There is no analogy. To say it is like a 'goal' in a game of football, doesn't help the 'explanatory process'. But you are not reduced to silence. In fact you explain things perfectly well. You explain, at this point, not the 'trick' so much as the whole game itself. You explain how the *game* is played. In the course of doing so, it becomes quite clear what a trick is.

So it is with the Resurrection. When you read all the accounts, you have an idea of what is being meant. And when you read about the Resurrection in the context of the whole Bible and its view of history, you understand more fully what it means.

Yes, we may have to talk about the Resurrection in paradoxical language sometimes. But we must expect to do that in borderland situations.

J. L. Austen, the Oxford linguistic philosopher, drew attention to this.[18] Here is a (far fetched) example: I turn up at your home just after a mutual friend who lives with you has dropped down dead and his corpse is still in the house. I ask, 'Is he at home?' What is the answer? 'He is and he isn't,' – you find it difficult answering in these terms. I ask further, 'What do you mean?' You then explain the sad event, and I understand. And I understand why a certain type of language doesn't fit. But if you *have* to speak in those terms – of 'being at home' – you *have* to speak paradoxically: 'He is both at home and not at home.'

Paradox and 'word failure' doesn't always imply unreality. Situations that defy language are not necessarily false or unhistorical. If the Bible is true and God is real, we will inevitably have these sorts of problems as we talk about God and his action in the world. It is unfortunate that we have to speak less clearly than we would like. This is only what you would expect if you have conceptual limitations. The Christian, though, says that one day it will make sense. 'Now we see in a mirror dimly, but then face to face. Now I know in part; then I shall understand fully' (1 Cor. 13.12).

It has been said more than once that the problems we face in talking about God and his working in the world are like the problems facing a map-maker. He has to map out in two dimensions something that is essentially three dimensional. The Christian similarly has to 'map out' something that is essentially eternal using the language that is fashioned for this world.

Donald Baillie puts it well: 'The attempt to put our experience of God into theological statements is something like the attempt to draw a map of the world on a flat surface, the page of an atlas. It is impossible to do this without a certain degree of falsification, because the surface of the earth is a spherical surface whose pattern cannot be reproduced accurately upon a plane. And yet the map must be drawn for convenience's sake. Therefore an Atlas meets the problem by giving us two different maps of the world which can be compared with each other. The one is contained in two circles, representing two hemispheres. The other is contained in an oblong (Mercator's projection). Each is a map of the whole world, and they contradict each other to some extent at every point. Yet they are both needed and taken together correct each other. They would be either misleading or mystifying to anyone who did not know that they represented the surface of a sphere.'[19]

Conclusion

The early Christians believed in an empty tomb because the tomb *was* empty. The resurrection of Jesus provides the only explanation of the 'emptiness' that is convincing. The resurrection appearances of Jesus were difficult to describe but not impossible to talk about.

7: Just a dream?

Appearances, visions and hallucinations

There are visionary experiences attested in most religious traditions. And it seems that the beliefs held determine the visions experienced. As Don Cupitt has pointed out: 'It's no accident that Catholics have visions of Mary, and Buddhists have visions of the Buddha, and not the other way round.'[1]

The resurrection appearances were not, however, quite like those sorts of visions. There was no belief to trigger them off. All the evidence shows that the disciples of Jesus had thought that he was quite literally dead and buried. They had to be *convinced* that he was alive.

The New Testament seems to distinguish the resurrection appearances from 'visions'. Luke is prepared to refer to the appearance of the angels at the tomb as 'visionary'. He reports the two on the road to Emmaus as referring to the women seeing a 'vision of angels' (Luke 24.23). But he reports the risen Jesus in person as saying, 'See my hands and my feet, that it is I myself; handle me, and see; for a spirit has not flesh and bones as you see that I have' (Luke 24.39).

Paul too distinguished his seeing Jesus on the Damascus Road from visionary experience. In his second epistle to the Corinthians he talks about such 'visionary experience' (12.1–4). He refers to 'visions and revelations of the Lord'. But he doesn't put these on a par with his 'seeing the Lord'. In his first epistle to the Corinthians he proves his apostleship by asking the question, 'Have I not *seen Jesus* our Lord?' (1 Cor. 9.1.).

In Paul's *visionary* experience he implies he was in something of a condition of heightened spiritual awareness – 'trance' is probably the wrong word. Paul doesn't really know how to put it: 'whether in the body or out of the body I do not know' (2 Cor. 12.2). Perhaps it was similar to Peter's 'consciousness' when in 'a trance' he had seen a 'vision' (Acts 11.5) or when once he was freed from prison through an angelic experience; he had to 'come to himself' when he got outside (Acts 12.11). Certainly John on the island of Patmos was 'in the spirit' when he had his 'vision' (Rev. 1.10).

But there was no suggestion with the resurrection appearances that they occurred when people were in a state of near-ecstasy. When Paul was on the way to Damascus he was not 'in the spirit' at all. Far from it. He was on a mission to exterminate Christians in a cold-blooded way!

We have to distinguish the resurrection appearances from visions. There was something 'public' and so 'objective' about the appearances of the risen Lord. When they occurred everyone present seemed to be aware of something. This was true of Paul's experience on the Damascus Road. The accounts of that occasion (Acts 9.1–8; 22.4–16; 26.9–18) are not particularly clear, but they make the point that those with Paul *also* heard or saw something. It wasn't an entirely private or subjective experience to Paul. Some have said that the resurrection appearances were subjective as they only occurred to believers. But of course that is not true; they occurred to unbelievers as well. Paul and James, the brother of Jesus, were both outside the Christian community when Jesus appeared to them.

'Visions', by contrast, in the Bible are more subjective and personal. More often than not they occur to one person; they may even be associated with 'dreaming'; 'And the Lord said to Paul one night in a vision . . .' (Acts 18.9). However, 'visions' can be of two sorts in the Bible – 'true' or 'false': there can be 'lying visions' as well as visions sent by God (Jer. 14.14). The belief here is that in a 'true vision' the subjective experience communicates a truth or a fact that God wishes to reveal; in a 'false vision' the source is not the inspiration of God, but what Jeremiah describes as 'the deceit of (men's) own minds' (Jer. 14.14).

So we ought to distinguish the resurrection appearances of Jesus from visionary experiences that are from God; and these in turn need to be distinguished from 'false' visionary experiences.

As the New Testament reports the 'seeing' of the risen Jesus it was not at all visionary or 'in the mind's eye'; he was 'out there' in the real world. While we may call visions subjective experiences, we cannot call this 'seeing' of Jesus subjective.

'But,' asks someone, 'can we really make all these distinctions? Why not use Augustine's threefold types of vision – 'corporeal', 'imaginary' and 'intellectual'? Anyhow, aren't we just talking about 'hallucinations'? And can we really lump Paul's experience on the Damascus Road with the Easter experiences of the disciples? They read so differently.'

Hallucinations

Let's take the last part of that question first. Can we really put Paul's experience alongside the experience of the disciples who saw Jesus before his ascension? They seem so unlike. The 'light from heaven' and 'a voice' that Paul saw and heard (Acts 9.3–4) are different from the figure who 'stood on the beach' (John 21.4).

True, but Paul himself was convinced that this was a resurrection appearance as was the early church. It was 'last of all, as to one untimely born' (1 Cor. 15.8); and unlike his visionary experiences Paul was prepared to *speak* about this 'seeing of Jesus'.

If, then Paul's experience is to be linked to experiences of the other disciples before Pentecost, how can we explain the differences? We don't know. But we could conjecture.

The 'form' in which the risen and exalted Jesus manifested himself to his disciples was the one best suited to assure them of his resurrection from the dead. The basic series of initial resurrection appearances were to enable Jesus' own disciples to realise that the Lord they thought was dead was alive in a new way; the one they 'had hoped . . . to redeem Israel' (Luke 24.21) and was buried had risen. They knew he had died; they had to be convinced he was alive. The 'bodily' manifestations assured them of this and the nature of his resurrection.

But Paul had to be convinced of something *more* than the 'aliveness' of Jesus and his resurrection. He had never yet submitted to Jesus as his master, as the disciples had done during

Jesus' earthly ministry. Paul had to know that Jesus was not only risen but also the redeemer. He needed to know that Christ was on the throne and reigning as the Lord. Perhaps that accounts for the differences. Perhaps the appearance to James, the brother of Jesus, was similar to Paul's. He too was another unbeliever who had to be convinced of both the fact that Jesus had risen and was indeed Christ, the Lord.

Were *all* of these experiences hallucinations?

It is very hard to say that the resurrection appearances could have been hallucinatory. They occurred to so many different types of people. We would have expected more of a 'stereotyped' set of people to have been involved had they been hallucinations. Then we would have expected them to have occurred in more uniform settings. Again, why, when so many people seem to have been involved, did they all suddenly stop after a period of forty days?

'Hallucination' in any case is an imprecise term. It certainly is when used with regard to the resurrection appearances, or even visions. When used of 'visions' it is to prejudge them.

Visions have occurred and do occur in the history of religious experience. In Norwich, an English city with strong religious associations, Julian had sixteen visions on 8 May 1373. More recently there has been an instance of 'group' visions.

In Fatima, a small town in the middle of Portugal, on 13 May 1917, three illiterate children saw a 'vision' of Mary who reappeared on five subsequent occasions. On the last occasion she said she was 'Our Lady of the Rosary' and asked for a chapel to be built in her honour.

But however you think of that, as true 'vision' or hallucination, it doesn't compare with the collective 'seeings of Jesus'. Matthew, Mary, Thomas and Peter, for a start, were such a diverse bunch of people. For them to have had a similar psychological make-up goes against all the evidence. These three girls at Fatima were all of the same background and near to each other in age. They all came from a simple Roman Catholic tradition. They already believed in Mary as the 'mother of God'. A 'vision' of her as a supernatural person could have been triggered off by belief. But as we have said this could not have happened like that with the disciples. They had *lost* their belief in Jesus. It certainly could not have happened with Paul and James who had never had a belief in Jesus.

Some hallucinations are apparently triggered off by visual signals. You see one thing and are convinced that it is something else. 'A hallucination means seeing something else, and mistaking it for what you are looking for.'[2] But in the New Testament record of the resurrection appearances you get the very opposite of that. Mary did not see the gardener near the tomb and think he was Jesus. She saw Jesus and thought he was the gardener. The two on the road to Emmaus did not see a stranger and think he was Jesus. They saw Jesus and thought he was a stranger. The apostles in the upper room did not see a ghost and think it was Jesus. They saw Jesus and thought they had seen a ghost.

Nor is there the slightest evidence that the disciples had 'unhinged' personalities. A number were tough fishermen, who appear to have been interested in getting back to business as soon as possible after the Resurrection (John 21.3). They were tough enough to withstand persecution for Jesus sake, even going to prison and being flogged for his sake.

Why not then take the New Testament records at their face value? Why not admit that the easiest explanation of the experiences is that they were of the risen Jesus who was real, objective and indeed inaugurating the beginning of the new Age? God had indeed 'visited' and redeemed his people. The appearances, coupled with the empty tomb, proved what had happened.

'We can't,' some say, 'because of the problem of the *location* of these appearances as recorded in the Gospels.'

The place

A new science is being born: it is called 'human ethology'. For some time researchers have realised that 'territory' is important for animals; they are now saying it is important for human beings. We all like and need our places. 'They influence the form and nature of our social contacts. They influence our feelings of identity and self-worth.[3] 'Surely,' the sceptic says, 'this is the reason why the Gospel narrative makes Jesus "appear" in different places. People associated with Jerusalem in the south wanted to claim the risen Jesus as their own; so they made the resurrection appearances occur in Jerusalem. People from northern Palestine wanted Jesus as their own. They put his resurrection appearances in Galilee.'

The reason why there is felt to be a conflict in the New Testament evidence is this: Luke and John, it is said, describe appearances of Jesus in Jerusalem, while Matthew and Mark imply Galilean appearances.

But that is to overstate the problem. Those who try to see two mutually exclusive resurrection traditions often fail to point out these important facts: John did not only record the Jerusalem appearances in chapter 20. He also wrote an 'appendix' (chapter 21) which clearly records an appearance of Jesus by the sea of Galilee in the North. That was when Jesus spoke to Peter about 'love'. And Matthew did not only speak about Jesus in Galilee (Matt. 28.16), he quite clearly says that Jesus appeared to the women on the first Easter day, which was of course in Jerusalem (Matt. 28.8–10).

Luke, in fact, is the only problem. He does not record any Galilean appearances. He also records the risen Jesus as saying 'stay in the city' (Luke 24.49).

But we need to remember that the Gospel writers were selective. They chose to record events in the light of an overall purpose. Luke is clearly wanting to emphasise Jerusalem. He may well have known of the Galilean appearances; but he chose to stress the Jerusalem appearances. His Gospel, and the end part of his Gospel, has to be read in conjunction with the book of Acts. One theme of Acts is the story of how the Christian Church was not just some tiny Judaean sect, but a faith fit for the Roman empire and the centres of power. It is the story of how the gospel went from Jerusalem to Rome and beyond. It is the story of witnesses 'in Jerusalem and in all Judea and Samaria and to the end of the earth' (Acts 1.8). As for the command of Jesus that the Apostles should stay in Jerusalem until they were 'clothed with power from on high' (Luke 24.49) this looks like a command from the time of the Ascension. If so, it doesn't tell us anything about the whereabouts of the disciples between Easter and the Ascension. In fact the command to stay in the city implies that normally at festival times the disciples' habit was to leave Jerusalem soon after the end of the festival. If this

command was given in the Pentecost season, it suggests that the
disciples had left Jerusalem after Passover (and the Resurrection)
and had gone back to Galilee.

Of course, Luke may not have known of appearances in
Galilee, but that doesn't prove they didn't take place there *and*
in Jerusalem.

The sequence

Indeed, Professor C. F. D. Moule of Cambridge asks: 'Is it so
impossible . . . to conceive of appearances taking place first in
Jerusalem and then in Galilee – possibly, then once again in
Jerusalem?'[4] Of course not!

We must remember that the eleven disciples were all from
Galilee or with northern connections themselves. They had come
down to Jerusalem for the Passover festival as Jesus had. But at
festival times the city was crowded with visitors and it was
difficult to find a place to stay. Jesus we know often stayed outside
the city with his friends at Bethany. Because of accommodation
problems at the best of times, it is most likely therefore that most
of the disciples would have returned home to their families and
friends in Galilee. That would have been the natural thing to
have done. If they did so, why could they not then have seen
Jesus up in the North. If as it seems, the appearances of Jesus
extended over a certain period of time, it is indeed highly likely
that he was *also* seen in Galilee, as well as initially in Jerusalem.
The disciples would have stayed in Galilee until the next festival,
the festival of Pentecost for which they would have had to travel
back to Jerusalem.

We tend to forget that Palestine is a very small country. Galilee
is only about sixty miles from Jerusalem. We are not talking of
a journey from Edinburgh to London and certainly not from
New York to Los Angeles! 'To-ing' and 'fro-ing' was not at all
impossible on foot. This was the way most would have travelled.

So when the disciples returned to Jerusalem for Pentecost after
several weeks break, why should not some of them have seen
Jesus again in Jerusalem? Indeed, if the Ascension is true, they
must have.

All this makes eminent sense of the texts. Mark reports the

message: 'he is going before you to Galilee' (Mark 16.7). This seems to suggest that the disciples were told to expect to find Jesus already there in Galilee when they returned home. And the command in Luke and Acts (not to leave Jerusalem after Pente-cost but to wait) was given, as we have said, *for this very reason*, namely that after the last festival, the Passover, that is just what they hadn't done – stayed in Jerusalem! (Luke 24.49; Acts 1.4)!

Why should the appearances of Jesus all be in one place? Some may assume that that was the case because often in the history of visionary experience such experiences have been associated with one place, as was the case at Fatima. But what if the resurrection appearances of Jesus were not on a par with these sort of experiences? The fact that they were not all associated with one place is every reason to view them as something quite different and distinct.

Predictions

Some doubt the reality of the resurrection appearances because of the predictions Jesus made about his death and resurrection during his ministry.

According to the Gospels Jesus had predicted his resurrection. Therefore, the sceptic says, the disciples *were* equipped with a set of beliefs that could have triggered off 'visionary experiences' of the risen Jesus. But the trouble with that suggestion is that in the Gospel accounts the disciples failed to understand the refer-ences to Jesus death, let alone his resurrection. They couldn't believe in a dying Messiah.

Some of course would not find the 'predictions' a problem. They would deny that they could possibly have influenced the disciples because Jesus never actually made them.

Well, did Jesus predict that he would die and rise again, or are the Gospel writers simply adding on 'bits and pieces' in the light of subsequent events?

No one can deny that Jesus predicted his *death*, although some would no doubt prefer the word 'premonition'. It is unthinkable that Jesus' words to Peter when he rebuked him – 'Get behind me, Satan!' (Mark 8.33) – were an addition after the death and resurrection of Jesus. They would not have been invented in the days of the growth of the church and the leadership of Peter.

These words were uttered in the context of a prediction. Jesus was saying that he would die, and rise again. Peter obviously was reacting to the idea of a dying Messiah. We are told that 'Peter took him (Jesus), and began to rebuke him' (Mark 8.32). And that is when Jesus in turn rebuked Peter.

So at least Jesus must have predicted his death. But if that is the case why could he not have predicted his resurrection as Mark tells us he did: 'And he began to teach them that the Son of man must suffer many things, and be rejected by the elders and the chief priests and the scribes, and be killed, and after three days rise again' (Mark 8.31).

Notice that Jesus uses the term 'Son of man' to make this prediction. New Testament criticism has shown us that 'Son of man' is never a term used by men to refer to Jesus in his earthly ministry. It is only used by Jesus to refer to himself. But 'the idea that it is as the Son of man that he must suffer and die and rise again is so novel that *it can only have arisen in the mind of Jesus.*'[5]

According to Daniel chapter 7 verses 13 and 14 the Son of man was a heavenly supernatural figure. He was to come from heaven with power and glory. So when Jesus spoke of the Son of man coming 'in the glory of his Father with the holy angels' (Mark 8.38) the disciples would have known what he was talking about and felt at home. When he spoke of the Son of man dying, they could not cope. But if they could not understand his death, how much less would they have understood talk about his resurrection *from the dead.*

These predictions, therefore, that are recorded both in the synoptic gospels and John, could not have acted as a trigger for 'visionary experiences'.

'But,' someone says, 'isn't there *some* evidence that the predictions were understood? Can we be so sure that the disciples didn't understand?'

It is true that Matthew implies that the *Jewish* leaders were aware of these predictions. That is why they asked for a guard at the tomb. They did not want the disciples to steal the body of Jesus and claim a 'resurrection'. They had 'resurrection worries'

(Matt. 27.63–4). And we must take this guard seriously. Some don't. For Pilate's refusal to provide a Roman guard and his insistence that the Jewish authorities use the temple police rings true to the political realities. After Joseph's request from Pilate for the body, it was now back in Jewish custody. Pilate wanted to make sure that 'responsibility for any riots that might ensue would fall fairly and squarely upon Jewish shoulders.'[6]

But if the Jewish opponents of Jesus understood something of his predictions, why then didn't the disciples understand? The answer is because the disciples believed he was the Messiah and the Son of man; so the idea of his dying even with his rising was anathema to them. And you hear what you want to hear. The Jewish opponents of Jesus, of course, had no such beliefs. They did not believe that he was the Messiah or the Son of man and so were quite open, if not happy, to hear predictions of death; and in that context they heard predictions of resurrection.

'Remember,' says James Martin, 'that the Jewish leaders in contrast to the disciples had their wits about them at this time; they were doing something desperate which might prove their undoing, and they could not afford to risk a mistake. Consequently it is altogether likely that *they* thought a great deal about the claims of Jesus at the very time when the *disciples* had dismissed them from their minds through grief and fear.'[7]

Conclusion

The resurrection appearances were not 'visions'; nor was there anything to 'trigger' them off, not even Jesus' predictions about his death and resurrection – these were not sufficiently understood by the disciples. There is no reason why Jesus could not have been 'seen' both in Galilee and Jerusalem.

8: The Church of Jesus Christ

The growth of the Church

The fact of the Church today is one of the unquestionable 'evidences' for the resurrection of Jesus Christ. The Church proves that the kingdom of God has begun in the Resurrection, even though it awaits a consummation one day.

Amazing things are happening in the Church in the world today. The Church is growing. This growth is not in Western Europe, the scene of the earliest expansion of Christianity, but in other parts of the world. Peter Wagner, an authority on 'Church Growth' at Fuller Theological Seminary in California, says this: 'I am often amused by Christians who are overly nostalgic. They say, "My, the Christian Church is in terrible shape. If we could only get back to the first century, we would know what God really can do through a dedicated church." I don't think we're perfect today by any means, but I disagree with that perspective. I honestly think that if Luke himself could have the choice, he would rather live today than in the first century. When we lift up our eyes to what God is doing *world wide* today, that activity around the eastern Mediterranean seems like a small pilot project compared to what is happening now.'[1]

There is church growth in some places in North America. But it is in Latin or South America that remarkable things have been happening this century.

In 1900 there were 50,000 Protestants in Latin America.[2] By 1970 there were 20 million; by 1980 there were 50 million and the Roman Catholic Church is experiencing a renewal as well. It is interesting to note: 'Some people thought that Marxism would defeat Christianity in Latin America. Although it is true that Marxism is very strong all over the Continent, no such defeat has occurred. In Chile, for example, where the first freely elected Marxist president in the world was in control, the churches were not hindered one bit in the aggressive evangelism that has characterised them through the years. In many cases, it seems as though the social revolution makes people more open than ever before to the claims of Christ.'[3]

Africa shows a similar story. In 1900 on the basis of those who say they are Christian there was 1 Christian in Africa to 28 non-Christians. By 1975 on a similar basis there was 1 Christian to 2.5 non-Christians. And much of this growth has been since the 'colonial period' has ended. In Africa it is now estimated that the Church is growing by six million a year!

In parts of Asia (including China) there is also growth. The Protestant Church in Indonesia has grown from 500,000 in 1910 to 6 million in 1975, with many converted from Islam. At the World Council of Churches Assembly in Uppsala in 1968 an Indonesian delegate was depressed by Western Christian leaders. 'I do not know why so doleful a picture of the church is being given,' he said. 'In my country so many people are clamouring to enter the Christian Church that we do not know how quickly enough to prepare them for baptism or how adequately to receive them into the Christian fellowship.'

Korea is witnessing, perhaps, the most interesting growth of all. In 1966 11 per cent of the Korean population were Christian. By 1978 it was 19 per cent. In 1981 it was 22 per cent.

Is this all the result of a delusion? Or is it the power and presence of the risen Christ in his Church that is the cause of it? The fact of the Church cannot be ignored as we consider the question of the resurrection of Jesus. In the last part of the twentieth century the impact of the Church is more significant than ever. Bishop Stephen Neil, the expert on missionary affairs, has taken a sweeping look at the current situation. He has observed 'never in human history has there ever been what might be classified as a universal religion, until today. We now have one that qualifies, and that religion in Christianity![4]

The beginnings

Apart from the Resurrection, how on earth can you account for what happened at the beginning?

Here were the disciples, as we have seen, terrified lest they would be taken prisoners like Jesus had been. They, therefore, didn't want to be too identified with Jesus. Peter even denied that he knew Jesus (Mark 14.71). None of them were prepared to carry Jesus' cross or risk asking for his body for burial. As we have seen that was left to a member of the Sanhedrin who had less to fear from Pilate or the Jews (Mark 15.43). Then it was the women followers of Jesus who went to the tomb on that Easter morning. The men seemed to have been in hiding, 'for fear of the Jews'.

But then all was changed. Now Peter was defying the authorities; a short while before he had denied he had any connection with Jesus. When they told him to stop preaching about Jesus and his resurrection, he, together with John replied: 'Whether it is right in the sight of God to listen to you rather than to God, you must judge; for we cannot but speak of what we have seen and heard' (Acts 4.19–20). He now not only risked imprisonment; he was imprisoned.

Before long this little group of disciples began to grow as you can read in the Acts of the Apostles. There were 120 (Acts 1.15), then 3,000 (Acts 2.41), then 5,000 (Acts 4.4). Like all growing churches they experienced 'growth problems'. Because they 'were increasing in number', they had to appoint seven more full-time workers. Then, as a result, we read: 'the number of disciples multiplied greatly in Jerusalem, and a great many of *the priests* were obedient to the faith' (Acts 6.1,3,7).

Some of 'the priests' started to be converted. James Martin reminds us how remarkable this in itself is: 'They were "in the know". That is to say, they had all the information as it was represented from the enemy's side, and were acquainted with all the best anti-resurrection arguments and theories. Pre-disposed in every way to reject the Christian claim, they were perhaps the least likely people to be converted to belief that history has ever known. Yet many of them were converted.'[5]

Then as you read on in the Acts of the Apostles you find that

Saul of Tarsus, a great intellectual and totally opposed to the message of the Resurrection, is converted. He gets the new name of 'Paul' and is himself responsible for the outreach to Europe.

He had a vision while in Troas of a man asking him to sail the Aegean sea and visit Philippi in Macedonia (Acts 16.9). He did so. That was perhaps one of the most momentous events in the history of the Christian Church. 'When St Paul sailed from Troy,' writes Christopher Dawson, 'in obedience to a dream and came to Philippi in Macedonia, he did more to change the course of history and the future of European culture than the great battle which had decided the fate of the Roman Empire on the same spot more than ninety years before.'[6]

Yet Paul personally got no material satisfaction out of what he did. He was hardly noticed, at the time; and when he was, he was pronounced a trouble maker. All that we know for sure of that visit to Philippi in terms of success was that the mob attacked him, he was sent to prison and made three converts. There was a business woman from Asia Minor, a slave girl who was mixed up in the occult and a prison officer (with his family) (Acts 16.11–40). So what was Paul's motivation? Why do and endure all this? His own answer was in terms of the Resurrection, as he was to tell these same Philippians some time later after the church there had been planted and grown. He wrote to them saying that the driving force in his own life was 'that I may know (Christ) and the power of his resurrection, and may share in his sufferings, becoming like him in his death, that if possible I may attain the resurrection from the dead' (Phil. 3.10–11).

Sunday

When Paul had first visited Philippi the first thing he did was to search out a group of people who he thought would be meeting for prayer 'on the sabbath day' (Acts 16.13). These would have been people interested in the Jewish faith in some way or another – 'God-fearers'. And they met on the Sabbath (or Saturday) because that was the day for Jewish worship. But before long we find Christians meeting together on Sunday. The next time we read of Paul at Troas, we find he is meeting with the Christians there 'on the first day of the week' when they gathered to 'break bread' (Acts 20.7). Why this change if there was no Resurrection?

We don't know for sure when the Christians first set apart the first day of the week as a special day for worship. From the record in Acts it seemed that the disciples in Jerusalem still followed the traditional practices for a period after Pentecost. They obviously still worshipped at the Temple. In fact they would have appeared to be just another of the Jewish sects. They were distinguished by their teaching on the Messiah and the Resurrection. Like Paul after his conversion they would have been known at first as the ones who went round 'proving that Jesus was the Christ (Messiah)' (Acts 9.22). We may assume that they would have still continued to observe the seventh day as a day of rest.

However the early Christians were marked off by one other thing – a special practice – the breaking of bread. This was not part of the temple worship; rather it was for those who 'devoted themselves to the apostles' teaching and fellowship' (Acts 2.42). It was something they did on their own without the rest of the Jews being present. Before long we find that *this* is taking place in Troas 'on the first day of the week'. Remember Eutychus? He was at that meeting. Paul was going on and on! Eutychus, like a number after him, fell asleep during the sermon. Unfortunately he was in the window seat and fell out – on the Sunday. The Corinthian Church also met on a Sunday. 'On the first day of every week, each of you,' writes Paul, 'is to put something aside and store it up' (1 Cor. 16.2). He was referring to money. This was something else they were to do on a *Sunday*.

Perhaps this development of the use of Sunday took quickest root in the Gentile churches, like those at Troas and Corinth. We don't know. But why the change from Saturday to Sunday, from the seventh to the first day of the week? Why did the Christians set aside the first day of the week instead of following the traditional Jewish pattern? There must have been something of great importance. The Christians did not choose to alienate the Jews. In fact, so far as they could they tried to live at peace with all men.

The resurrection of Jesus is the only satisfactory answer. This was something big enough to give rise to the change. This was the answer the early Christians gave. An early bishop, Ignatius from Antioch, spoke about 'no longer observing sabbaths but fashioning . . . lives after the Lord's day, on which our life also rose through him.'[7] At the end of the first century AD or the beginning of the second Sunday worship was fully established. In the *Didache* (from that time) we read: 'On the Lord's own day gather yourselves together and break bread and give thanks, first confessing your transgressions.'[8]

And of course celebration of Sunday 'the third day', presupposes an empty tomb. It was on the third day the tomb was found empty. Visions alone would not give rise to Sunday. They were not unique to the first day of the week.

Suffering

Belief in the Resurrection has gone hand in hand with the experience of suffering. The expansion of the church has not been without pain. But suffering has not been able to erase this central belief of the Christian faith. Indeed 'the blood of the martyrs is the seed of the Church'. Perhaps for many it is this ability to live through suffering that is the greatest witness to the Resurrection. In this century alone it has been estimated that more Christians have died for their faith *than in all the preceding Christian centuries*.

If you ask the question 'why have Christians died for their faith?', the answer must be 'because of the Resurrection'. The one thing that marks off Christianity from every other religion or philosophy is the resurrection of Jesus Christ. To a degree you can find parallels for the ethics of Christianity in other religions and philosophies. People would not originally have been won to Jesus Christ because of the Sermon on the Mount alone. The conviction that Jesus rose from the dead was and is central. As one New Testament scholar has said: 'What has to be given some account of in the Christian movement is that it appears to have had no distinctive advantage to offer or novelty to proclaim *except* that one, preposterous, conviction; and it was this conviction, tenaciously maintained, that (against their will) squeezed Christians out of the Synagogue as no other Jewish heresies seem to have done.'[9]

Let's be specific and for a moment take a look at a 'suffering church' and see how important to it the Resurrection is. We have a cameo of such a church in the book of Revelation; the church is the Church of Smyrna referred to in chapter 2. And the message it is being reminded of is the message of the Resurrection. In John's vision the author of all 'seven letters' (seven churches are being written to) is the risen Jesus (Rev. 1.18). Yet the Church of Smyrna needs to be reminded of this more than the others; so the introduction of the letter is in the following form: 'The words of the first and the last, who died and came to life' (Rev. 2.1). What was the problem?

Smyrna was a splendid city of Asia Minor, north of Ephesus. It was proud of its Roman connection and not surprisingly, therefore, it was a centre of emperor worship. Each year the citizens would be asked to parade before a bust of the emperor by which a small fire was burning and then sprinkle a pinch of incense into the fire and say 'Caesar is Lord'.

It was quite a wealthy city and it had a significant Jewish community. We know very little about the Church there. The New Testament does not tell us how or when it was founded. We don't know the names of its leaders or who brought the gospel first to Smyrna. But we do know that the Christians at Smyrna suffered for their faith and this suffering was intense. The text calls it 'tribulation' (Rev. 2.9). Perhaps it had to do with the emperor cult. Perhaps it was because they refused to say, as we know they refused to say, 'Caesar is Lord'. They could only say, 'Jesus is Lord'. And their refusal to conform or to fit in with the other citizens of Smyrna led to trouble for them. They were seen as a dissident group having a treacherous lack of patriotism. So they were persecuted and suffered. But they were being misunderstood. They were not at all unpatriotic or treacherous. It was simply that Jesus Christ was their Lord and he demanded their first loyalty.

This has been the 'way' for countless Christians down the centuries – suffering and misunderstanding. Many will remember the fact that the Anglican Bishop in Iran had his secretary shot and his son murdered? Why? Because he was a Christian and not a Muslim and because he was no doubt misunderstood. In an Islamic state being a Christian may be thought to be unpatriotic.

The ultimate sacrifice

In addition to being persecuted and misunderstood, the Church at Smyrna experienced poverty. 'Make no mistake;' writes one commentator on this little epistle to the Smyrneans, 'it does not always pay to be a Christian. Nor is honesty by any means always the best policy, if material gain is your ambition. Poverty has often been part of the cost of Christian discipleship.'[10] Perhaps the poverty of the Christians in Smyrna ('I know your tribulation and poverty . . . and the slander' (Rev. 2.9)) was connected with the fact that they were straight in business. Perhaps they refused some shady methods that would have given quick profits. Perhaps they were not given business contracts because they took a stand over not sacrificing to the emperor.

But there was worse in store than poverty. In the letter they were warned: 'Behold, the devil is about to throw some of you into prison, that you may be tested' (Rev. 2.10). Imprisonment was to follow poverty. Again this has been an experience common to many Christians. Throughout the history of the Christian Church there have been those who have tried to suppress the message of the Resurrection by imprisonment. From the Apostle Peter to Richard Wurmbrand and countless others in totalitarian regimes of both the right and the left, prison has been a weapon used against the Church. And beyond prison is execution.

Sometimes the Christian is called to the ultimate sacrifice for the one he or she believes is risen. 'Be faithful,' the Christians at Smyrna were told, *'unto death'* (Rev. 2.10). As we have noted there have been many martyrs this century. I had the privilege of working in the Sudan in the mid-sixties. It was a time of devastation in the South, where the majority of Sudan's Christians live. Schools, churches and hospitals were destroyed, and Christians brutally killed. The mission centre I was attached to was burnt to the ground and totally destroyed. There is a cost in discipleship, as the Christians at Smyrna were to learn.

One of the greatest Christian Martyrs was one day to come from Smyrna, Bishop Polycarp. He was martyred probably in the year AD 156. He is bound to have meditated on these verses in the book of Revelation that make up this letter to the Church at Smyrna.

He refused to sacrifice to Caesar. His captors thought he was mad. 'What harm can it do to sacrifice to the emperor?' the officer asked. 'Swear by the genius of Caesar . . . Swear, and I will release you; revile Christ.'

But old Polycarp replied with those marvellous words: 'Eighty and six years have I served him, and he has done me no wrong; how then can I blaspheme my King who saved me?'

Soon he was to be burnt to death as a punishment for his confession of faith in the risen Jesus. As the flames were coming he prayed to God like this: 'I thank thee that thou hast thought me worthy, this day and this hour, to share the cup of thy Christ among the number of thy witnesses.'[11] How do you explain such a faith if it is all based on a series of hallucinations?

How do you explain the faith of those Southern Sudanese Christians? On one occasion when there was a respite in the fighting in the South Sudan, the Church Missionary Society's Africa Secretary was able to visit Juba Cathedral. He reported that it was most moving to hear the congregation of the packed Cathedral, many of whom had suffered terribly, singing the chorus, 'Yesterday today for ever Jesus is the same; all may change but Jesus never, glory to his name.'

Conclusion

The fact of the Church is a witness to the Resurrection. Its continuing growth, its worship 'on the first day', and its ability to withstand suffering and persecution are hard to explain if the resurrection of Jesus is not true.

9: Belief and doubt

Faith

At this point we need to change gear. We need to take stock and go back to some basics.

Few will deny that Jesus Christ, as the central figure in the Gospels, commands universal admiration and exerts an amazing power over people. Franco Zeffirelli, the film producer, produced the TV series on the Life of Christ, *Jesus of Nazareth*. He reported that when a rough cut of the film was shown, even the most hard boiled actors were in tears. Napoleon made a famous comparison between Christ and Alexander, Caesar, Charlemagne and himself: 'I think I understand something of human nature; and I tell you, all these were men, and I am a man: none else is like him!'

People are drawn by the life of Christ. The sticking point for so many modern men and women, certainly when life is comfortable, is the Resurrection. In the musical *Godspell*, a lively theatrical production on the life of Christ, the final number is 'long live God'. But he lives on 'long' not in the person of the risen Christ, but in the memories of the disciples; that is how the production I saw left things.

This is not New Testament Christianity as we have now seen; nor is it the Christianity that is a strength in suffering. Emphatically the early Apostles preached Jesus *and the Resurrection* (Acts 17.18). Listen to Peter, again from his Pentecost sermon: 'Brethren, I may say to you confidently of the patriarch David that he both died and was buried, and his tomb is with us to this day (i.e. there is a tomb to which pilgrimage can be made, and at which homage can be paid to the mortal remains of King David, but . . .) he (David) foresaw and spoke of the resurrection of the Christ, that he was *not* abandoned to Hades (the place of the dead) nor did his flesh see corruption (in thorough decomposition as David's did. No . . .). This Jesus God raised up, and of that we all are witnesses' (Acts 2.29, 31–2).

This was the message that turned the world upside down. A message about the resurrection of Jesus Christ. This was a real resurrection with an empty tomb.

But again we ask, after reviewing all the evidence, did it happen? How do we make up our minds?

From what we have said about history earlier we will not be surprised to find that there has to be an interaction between events and faith. And faith needs to be defined precisely to avoid misunderstanding. Christian faith is not a blind leap in the dark. It is based on facts and events. Yet such historical events by themselves will not necessarily create faith. For Christian faith is much bigger than mere knowledge of such facts. It is a thankful response of the whole being to God. But it has to rest on facts and events. If these are false, if what the witnesses claim to have happened, did not happen, that is the end. 'If Christ has not been raised, then our preaching is in vain and your faith is in vain . . . we are of all men most to be pitied' (1 Cor. 15.14, 19). So said Paul.

The question remains, how can we know? How can we make up our minds given all the arguments and all the evidence? Alan Richardson suggests two important factors. The resurrection has to be the best of all the explanations of the known facts; but it also has to fit in with our 'own deepest understanding and experience of life': 'Two conditions would have to be fulfilled before the judgment could be reached that the traces of the past point towards the resurrection of Christ as the most coherent explanation of the evidence. First, there would have to be credible attestation on the part of witnesses to happenings which could not be more rationally accounted for by some alternative hypothesis; and, secondly, the event attested would have to accord with the historian's own deepest understanding and experience of life.'[1]

Then, at that point you have to be prepared to 'commit yourself'. But this commitment is not *inspite of* the facts and evidence. Everything fits together. What is believed is not contradicted by the known facts. For that reason one important aspect of New

Testament scholarship and discussion about the New Testament is what Helmut Thielicke calls 'anti-criticism'. The New Testament scholar looks to see that there are no known facts that would disprove, for example, the Resurrection. He is therefore able to put forward the view that Jesus actually rose from the dead as the best explanation of all the data; and that data includes all one's experiences of life as well as the records of the Gospels.

Doubt

Perhaps we spend too long on why we should *believe*. Books are written on the 'evidence for the Resurrection'. That is good. But we should not only ask questions about 'belief'; we should ask just as searching questions about doubt.

In the Easter story in the Gospel, as recorded in John, Thomas is the 'doubter'. He simply could not believe in the resurrection of Jesus. The other disciples came to believe, but not Thomas. Why was this? Why could he not believe that Jesus had left the tomb empty on that first Easter Day?

John's Gospel supplies the answer. It was 'because he was not with them when Jesus came' (John 20.24). Thomas kept himself apart from the other disciples. He was absent when Jesus appeared.

This is still a fundamental cause of doubt – a person's separation from the Christian community or fellowship. If you keep away from where the Bible is intelligently and carefully preached, if you don't put yourself in the way of Christian literature that is positive and helpful, if you don't let other Christians help you with your queries and questions, don't be surprised if you find faith difficult! John Wesley used to say that there is no such thing as 'a solitary Christian' – with good reason. Charles Spurgeon used the analogy of the coal in the fire. While the coal is in the fire it can glow red hot. Take it out and lay it on the hearth and its incandescence will fade and in the morning it will be stone cold. The Christian is like the coal. The point is this: it is not just 'words' that lead a person to Jesus Christ. It more often than not is 'love'; and for that you need a community.

We don't just believe what we do on *purely* intellectual grounds. Of course if intellectual reasons are absent altogether, it will not be Christian believing, but superstition. That is why we have considered a lot of arguments already in this book. But our emotions are very important too. How we feel about something may very much affect what we believe about it. Dr Armand Nicholai of the Harvard Medical school goes so far as to say this: 'We like to think that our beliefs are based on a careful consideration of the evidence. This, of course, is seldom the case. What we currently know about the functioning of the mind indicates rather clearly that our belief as well as our behaviour is influenced more by how we feel than by what we think.'[2]

When we are outside an active Christian fellowship, it is so easy to drift from faith. C. S. Lewis once observed, 'If you examined a hundred people who had lost their faith in Christianity, I wonder how many of them would turn out to have been reasoned out of it by honest argument? Do not most people simply drift away?'[3]

Sadly, if you are working in a church, you see this happen to a number of people. The cares of the world, as Jesus put it in the Parable of the Sower (Mark 4.19), often are all that is needed to start the drift. This then leads to a creeping paralysis of faith.

This happened to Charles Darwin (of evolution fame): 'I gradually came to disbelieve in Christianity as a divine revelation . . . disbelief crept over me at a very slow rate, but was at last complete.'[4] The devil in Lewis's *The Screwtape Letters* puts it so well: 'The safest road to Hell is the gradual one – the gentle slope, soft underfoot, without sudden turnings, without milestones, without signposts.'[5]

Scepticism

In the Gospel narrative Thomas is not only absent when Jesus appears to the other disciples. He is unduly sceptical. 'Unless I see in his hands the print of the nails . . . *I will not believe*' (John 20.25). Subsequently Jesus was to say to Thomas, when eventually he appeared to him as the risen Lord, 'Blessed are those who have not seen and yet believe' (John 20.29). These are not irrational people. They want evidence, but they believe that they have *sufficient* evidence.

Thomas may have been unduly sceptical. He was able to assess the gullibility of his fellow disciples. He knew they were no fools. But he refused to believe. In fact he had a negative turn of mind. He could have put things positively rather than negatively. He could have said, 'I will believe, if I see in his hands the print of the nails.' His cast of mind made him focus on refusing faith – 'I will *not* believe . . . unless . . .'

It is not uncommon to be over-sceptical. There are some people who are always asking for evidence but are never open to conviction. The Pharisees in the New Testament were just like that. Unlike Thomas who in the end accepted the evidence and came to confess Christ in the words, 'My Lord and my God!' (John 20.28), they *never* accepted any evidence. And there were plenty of people of this sort in Jesus' day (and their successors are still with us). Jesus called them 'an evil and adulterous generation' (Matt. 12.39). They were always wanting a 'sign'. But they had signs enough. As Peter could say without fear of contradiction in the Pentecost sermon: 'Jesus was attested . . . by God with mighty works and wonders and signs' (Acts 2.22).

But many of the Jews simply didn't want to submit to Jesus Christ as Saviour and Lord. It was a question of the 'will', not the intellect.

There are of course *real* intellectual doubts. That is why we have to distinguish between those who have real intellectual problems from those who have rationalisations. As Os Guinness puts it: 'This is the point at which to separate those who are doubting because they need answers from those who are doubting because they need doubts.'[6]

Let's think of one real problem people have from time to time. This is over the nature of *proof*. 'How,' they ask, 'can you be *really* sure? Yes, the arguments given are very good, but can we be certain?' Like the sceptical philosopher Descartes, they might well ask the question, 'How can I know that I know that I know . . .?' That question need never stop!

The trouble often begins when we don't have a wide enough idea of what it means to 'prove' something. Too often we think exclusively of 'mathematical' proofs. Or we think of 'logical' proofs, where the meanings of the words almost ensure that a conclusion is right. 'All men are mortal, Scorates is a man, *therefore* Socrates is mortal.'

But this is only one sort of proving. We mustn't be held prisoner by it. There are all sorts of other ways we prove things. Two obvious examples. A Romeo *proves* his love for a Juliet in countless ways that have nothing to do with mathematical or logical proofs. St George *proved* his valour by slaying the dragon. Again that had nothing to do with mathematics or logic!

There is a range of methods by which we reach certainty – *enough* certainty. The important thing is to ask yourself two questions: 'Am I looking for the *appropriate* sort of proof?' and 'Am I aware of what is a *reasonable* amount of certainty?'

The simple fact is that in everything apart from what philosophers call 'necessary truths' – mathematical and logical truths – there is no such thing as 'absolute certainty' of a 'mathematical sort'. So what? Indeed, this is what makes life interesting. This is particularly true of human relationships. You only become certain about people as you get to know them. And, as has been well put, 'The appropriate way to assure yourself of the reality of persons is to meet them, not to try to prove them!'[7]

The Christian says it is a bit like that with the risen Jesus Christ. The more you have dealings with him, the more you develop a relationship with him, the more certain you become. That is not to say that Christians don't have questions and sometimes doubts. But they are *sufficiently* certain. This is not about everything. In many things 'now we see in a mirror dimly' (1 Cor. 13.12). However, over the essentials they are sufficiently certain to be able to love, serve and obey God.

Commitment

Some people will still doubt that Christian 'proving' and certainty is reasonable. They will put Christian believing in much the same class as the toss of a coin; heads I win, tails you lose. Its a matter of chance. Alan Watts says: 'Without any disrespect it must be said that Christianity is pre-eminently the gamblers' religion.'[8]

It was the seventeenth century Frenchman, Pascal, who originally used the analogy of 'gambling' in thinking of faith. He taunted the sceptics of his own day, who doubted the existence of God and the resurrection of Jesus Christ, over their reckless gambling habits. They were prepared, he said, to stake huge fortunes in their gambling with far less chance of being winners or 'proved right' in their bets than is the Christian in his beliefs.

Pascal certainly didn't mean, however, that Christian belief was merely a 'luckier' draw. He used the analogy of gambling and faith to emphasise commitment. ' "We cannot wait," he means to say, "until our reason has carefully weighed all the pros and cons, the less so since the existence of God can never be proved by reason alone. In the meantime we waste our life in indecision . . . Let us take the risk, therefore, let us boldly dare to believe, even though merely on the strength of a vague probability." '[9] The point is well made (even if we think that the probability is not vague but high). Practical decisions can't wait for ever. And a decision to follow Jesus Christ is a *practical* decision. It is going his way and not ours. We will *do* different things if we are Christians to what we would do if we aren't.

In many areas of life you can't remain uncommitted for ever! Sometimes you have to 'jump'. And even in situations where the evidence is strong and clear, you can always carry on asking questions to avoid commitment. But if you do sometimes you can 'miss the boat' (or train).

Imagine a rather odd person – odd because he wants one hundred per cent certainty – on a station platform. He wants to know when is his next train home. He asks the porter who tells him, '5.00 p.m.' But he wants to make *sure*; after all the porter may have got it wrong. So he goes back to the booking office and sees the official timetable. There it is – 5.00 p.m. However, he thinks: 'that might be a misprint' or 'they might have changed the schedules today. I better check with the stationmaster.' While doing so, he looks at his watch. It now says, 5.01 p.m. He looks back to the platform he was earlier standing on and there he sees the train slowly pulling out. He has missed it!

In practical situations you cannot remain uncommitted for ever.

Pessimism

Thomas was not only unduly sceptical or so he seems. He was also a pessimist. Earlier in his ministry Jesus had talked about going back at risk to Judea. Thomas had immediately said: 'Let us also go, *that we may die with him*' (John 11.16). True, he was prepared to face the cost of discipleship. Some of the other Apostles did not seem quite so bold. But there is more than a hint of a 'mood' here. Thomas was looking on the black side all right.

Was he depressive? People who are depressed or cannot see life as good are predisposed to believe the worst. If the gospel is 'good news', they will doubt it. They will find it hard to believe that death was defeated in Christ through his resurrection.

Today we live in a 'depressed' world. This hardly needs to be said. Turn to the world of painting and art. If it is true that 'art lays bare the collective soul of a generation', then the late twentieth century is certainly in need of some help. The story told here is one of 'disharmony, the meaninglessness of life, despair, degradation, hedonism and sadness.'[10] This is a world 'having no hope and without God' (Eph. 2.12). There is thus a psychological and cultural predisposition to doubt. But how foolish if that prevents us from looking at the facts.

There is without question a 'hunger for God' in the midst of all this despair and pessimism. Bel Mooney, for example, rejected the idea of God at the age of 16. She wrote an article about her beliefs. Under the adjoining photograph of herself was the following caption, 'Bel Mooney admits the devout sceptic's desire for God.'[11]

Her problem was the problem of suffering. But that still doesn't stop people like her from their quest for God. There is a basic restlessness that pushes them into asking further questions about God and the resurrection of Jesus Christ. This is inspite of the despair and pessimism. David Watson, drawing on his wealth of experience in missions and Christian festivals, says, 'I have learned that *most people, if not all, are basically hungry for God*, even when they show little sign of this on the surface.'[12]

In fact it is possible that much of the despair and frustration in the modern world is because people have lost their spiritual 'moorings'. The psychiatrist, Carl Jung, said that 'modern man was in search of a soul.' In the book of that title he made the following observation: 'During the past thirty years people from all the civilised countries of the earth have consulted me. I have treated many hundreds of patients . . . Among all my patients in the second half of life – that is over thirty five, there has not been one whose problem in the last resort was not that of finding a religious outlook on life.'[13]

No wonder more and more people are asking questions about Jesus Christ. No wonder there are more people like the Liverpool sculptor, Arthur Dooley. He was making a ten foot statue of the risen Christ and being interviewed about it on the radio. He was asked if he believed in the Resurrection. His reply was: 'I don't know whether it's true or not, but I'd like to believe it.'[14]

'I believe what I want to'

Here we can leave Thomas. He was not this sort of sceptic or doubter.

Some people don't *want* to believe. Robert Browning began his poem 'Easter Day' with the exclamation, 'How very hard it is to be a Christian.' Because it is hard, some people may prefer not to start. Michael Green cites Aldous Huxley as a good example of this sort of person. He is the 'type of atheist who is unwilling, on his own admission, to commit himself to the demands of Christian living.' So Huxley says: 'I had motives for not wanting the world to have a meaning; consequently assumed that it had none, and was able without any difficulty to find satisfying reasons for this assumption. The philosopher who finds no meaning in the world is not concerned exclusively with a problem in pure metaphysics; he is also concerned to prove that there is no valid reason why he personally should not do as he wants to do, or why his friends should not seize political power and govern in the way that they find most advantageous to themselves . . . For myself, the philosophy of meaninglessness was essentially an instrument of liberation, sexual and political.'[15]

There is a moral dimension to doubt. If there is no Resurrection, if you can tell yourself that, you can allow yourself all sorts of selfish indulgence. Paul said, 'If the dead are not raised, "Let us eat and drink, for tomorrow we die" ' (1 Cor. 15.32).

It is interesting to note that the exponents of meaninglessness have often been associated with decadence in terms of sexual morality. We saw that earlier in the case of Bertrand Russell. But this is not only a twentieth century phenomenon. Think

back to Catullus, the Roman poet. He was no pillar of sexual
virtue! He loved boys as well as women. At the same time as he
invites Lesbia, his girl friend, to ignore the traditions of the older
generation and 'love', he gives voice to ultimate despair. He
reckons that we might as well enjoy all now as it will be snatched
away from us when we die: 'When the sun sets, it sets to rise
again. But for us, when our brief day is over, there is one endless
night that we must sleep . . . *"nox est perpetua una dormienda"* –
as someone has said, "perhaps the most shattering line that has
ever been written." '

But the moral dimension over belief is not only an issue for
modern secular man or pagan Romans. It affects theologians and
what they believe and teach.

Some have a naive view that theologians and biblical scholars
are always thoroughly objective and neutral. They simply look
at, for example, the New Testament evidence on the Resurrection, and then put the 'jig-saw' together. That is all there is to
it. It is either a matter of straightforward discovery or of neutral
detective work. Not so!

A modern theologian

Karl Barth, one of the most famous theologians of the twentieth
century, proves the reality is very different.

At one time Karl Barth was a faithful follower of the liberal
nineteenth century theologians who had successfully de-gutted
the Christian gospel. They held that there was no heaven or hell,
sin or atonement and that Christ was not really divine. Adolf von
Harnack (1851–1930), of whom Barth was a pupil, was a good
example of these views. He believed that Christianity was a valu-
able religion; but it was to be summarised in two catch phrases,
'the Fatherhood of God' and 'the Brotherhood of man'.

'Let's not fuss about the Resurrection or questions about where
Jesus went. Forget the plain record of the Bible. Jesus himself
did not really believe he was the son of God. We don't need to
believe either. The idea that Christ was both God and man is too
complicated. Originally there was a simple Galilean gospel – 'the
religion *of* Jesus'. Then Paul came along and complicated it. He
made it into a 'religion *about* Jesus'. These were the sort of ideas

Karl Barth had absorbed as a student – a nineteenth century 'New Theology'.

But suddenly Karl Barth changed his mind. He rejected the liberal theology of the nineteenth century and did a complete 'U'-turn – some would say, too complete. Why did he change?

It was not that he first looked afresh at the New Testament evidence. That wasn't the first thing that happened. No! What happened was this: he discovered one day in August 1914 that almost all of his admired liberal Protestant teachers were supporting the war policy of Kaiser Wilhelm II. These theologians had signed a declaration issued by ninety-three German intellectuals supporting the Kaiser's policies. Among the signatories was none other than Adolf von Harnack. There were also others who were Barth's theological teachers.

Listen to how Karl Barth recalled this event in later years: 'Among the signatures I found to my horror the names of nearly all my theological teachers whom up to then I had religiously honoured. Disillusioned by their conduct, I perceived that I should not be able any longer to accept their ethics and dogmatics, their biblical exegesis, their interpretation of history; that at least for me the theology of the nineteenth century had no future.'[16] And so Barth changed his own views and theology.

Here if ever is ample evidence from one of the foremost theologians of the twentieth century that the views we come to about the Bible do not depend simply on what is said in the text. There is a moral dimension.

Conclusion

Christian 'belief' in Jesus and the Resurrection is not an irrational 'leap in the dark'. Nor is it a matter of cold logic. It involves a willingness to be committed and a level of moral integrity.

10: Where did Jesus go? – 'to the dead'

Death

So much for 'belief' and 'doubt'. We are now in a position when we can begin to answer our question, 'Where did Jesus go?' The evidence all points to the fact that on that first Easter morning the tomb was found empty. The tomb where his body had been laid no longer contained the body of Jesus, not because it was stolen or removed to another place, but because Jesus had risen from the dead!

But precisely where did Jesus go after Joseph of Arimathea had 'bought a linen shroud, and taking him down, wrapped him in the linen shroud, and laid him in a tomb which had been hewn out of the rock; and rolled a stone against the door of the tomb' (Mark 15.46)?

One answer that countless Christians give Sunday after Sunday as they recite the Apostles' Creed is that *'He descended to the dead.'* What does that mean?

We need first to think about death. Many people have not come to terms with death and dying in this last part of the twentieth century. When there was a proposal to set up a hospice for the dying in one area of England not so long ago, there was some resistance. This was probably related to an unwillingness, probably subconscious, on the part of many people to face the reality of death.

For some death seems absurd and so they try to ignore it or laugh it away. Take one of the plays of Ionesco, *Amédée or How to get rid of it*. Here you have a play about a corpse that grows bigger and bigger until it floats away in the shape of a balloon – a balloon on the way to nowhere.[1]

Many people today say that death is meaningless, if not absurd.

They put on a cold front of realism and say that they have enough problems coping with life; 'we can't waste time on the problems of death.' One psychiatrist, however, thinks that people are worried deep down inspite of what they say: 'people today could be described as more realistic about death; but inside I think they are more afraid. Those old religious assurances that there would be a gathering-in some day have largely been discarded, and I see examples all the time of neuroses caused by the fear of death.'

We can, of course, forget death until we are ill or old. This is odd as we see so much of death and dying on our TV screens. But in some ways it is then at a distance from us. It isn't really in our living room! It is not immediate.

So much dying in the modern western world is in the geriatric ward of our local hospital anyhow. It is then anaesthetised and off stage; and that is why so many know only a little about death and dying and having seldom seen a real dead body. 'Children of the TV generation,' writes an American commentator, 'are such strangers to natural death that on hearing that grandfather is dead, they have been known to ask, "Who shot him?" '

But the New Testament puts death on the centre of the stage. It spends a great deal of its space talking about the death of Jesus. It says death is real. Dying is real; and sometimes dying can be terrifying, as it was for Jesus on the cross. Yet the good news of the Christian gospel is this: yes, death is terrible; but Jesus Christ became man 'that through death he might destroy him who has power of death, that is the devil, and deliver all those who through fear of death were subject to life long bondage' (Heb. 2.14–15).

One of the great consequences of the death and resurrection of Jesus is the hope and assurance they bring. That Jesus descended to the dead is one element in this assurance as we shall see. So then what does it mean?

Hades and Hell

Peter said on the day of Pentecost: '(David) foresaw and spoke of the resurrection of the Christ, that he was not abandoned to Hades, nor did his flesh see corruption' (Acts 2.31). If Christ was not abandoned to Hades, he went there first! But what is 'Hades' and how does it differ from 'Hell'?

The traditional versions of the Apostles' Creed, that some still use, have 'he descended *into hell*' rather than 'to the dead' or 'to hades'. 'Hell' is misleading, as English meanings have changed since these early translations. Originally 'hell' was used to translate *two* distinct words in the Greek text of the New Testament. It no longer is. The result has been some confusion.

The two distinct words are *Gehenna* and *Hades*. Each of these words has its roots in the Old Testament. *Gehenna* is the valley of Hinnom, the refuse dump outside Jerusalem where the garbage was burned. It had been the place of idolatrous child sacrifice. Its meaning was then extended to include the place of final retribution for sinners – 'hell' as we understand it today.

Hades is very different. It is *Sheol* of the Old Testament, the place of the departed. It refers to the whole of the unseen world that, it was believed, we pass into at death.

Gehenna is a place of punishment. Jesus said: 'If your right hand causes you to sin, cut it off and throw it away; it is better that you lose one of your members than that your whole body go into hell (*gehenna*)' (Matt. 5.30). *Hades* is more neutral. It is a place of waiting. Both the good and the bad are there according to the Old Testament.

The problem is that in normal modern usage 'hell' is always used to refer to the state of final punishment only; so it translates now *Gehenna* only. In the Creed, as in Peter's Pentecost sermon, it is said that *Jesus went not to Gehenna but to Hades*. That is why modern versions of the Apostles' Creed have not that Jesus 'descended into Hell', instead they have, 'he descended to the dead'. And that is right.

So what is meant is simply this: Jesus went through death into the unseen beyond the grave.

But how can we say today that Jesus *descended* to the dead? Isn't this pure mythology? Isn't such a doctrine a 'fantastic dream' – as F. W. Beare says: 'nothing else than the appropriation, and the application to Christ, of a fragment of the redemption-mythology of the Oriental religions, best known to us in the ancient story of the Descent of Ishtar to the underworld, and reflected also in a number of Greek myths (Orpheus and

Eurydice, Heracles and Alcestis, the story of Persephone, etc.)?'
And Beare adds that these are all 'rooted in vegetation- and sun-
myths'.[2]

Well, what do we say? Is it mythology?

Mythology

A great deal of confusion had often come over the use of the
word 'mythology'. It means different things to different people.

How can we define 'mythology'? Rudolph Bultmann, who has
used the word very freely and in so doing has greatly influenced
twentieth century Protestant academic theology, once defined it
like this: 'Mythology is the use of imagery to express the other-
worldly in terms of this world and the divine in terms of human
life, the other side in terms of this side.'[3]

Few would find fault with that use of the word 'mythology'.
Maybe the word is dangerous as suggesting 'fairy stories' or
'myths' like the ones Beare refers to; but *if the word is used in
this technical and sophisticated way*, we can see a lot of what
Christians say is 'mythological'. To say God is 'Our Father' is
mythological in this sense. For we don't mean that God is exactly
like a human father. We can't ask, for example, who is his
wife? We simply mean, and the Bible means, that God exhibits
'fatherly' characteristics. But he is not a 'literal' father in the way
a human being can be. We are simply 'expressing the other
worldly in terms of this world.' And from what we have seen
earlier this will certainly be necessary when talking about God.
Why then has there been such a great controversy over the
question of 'myth' in Christianity?

The problem came from Bultmann himself. Yet the problem
is not because of Bultmann's view of the way religious language
works. The problem came over what he is saying religious
language *refers* to. For he says that our religious language or our
biblical 'mythology' is mostly referring to man and not God and
the world. A great many of the religious statements about Christ
the eternal word, about his incarnation, about the reality of
demonic forces, about the Resurrection, Ascension and Last
Judgment are not statements about the way things happened or
are in the external world or will be one day, according to this

view. They are really statements about man's inner consciousness! Why? Because, said Bultmann, modern man cannot believe
in these things; you can't at one and the same time use electricity
and believe in the 'supernatural'. Why on earth not?

But we do need to be careful about the use of the word
'mythology' in connection with statements of belief.

It is often felt that a 'myth', even in this technical sense, is
something mysterious or uncertain; to use a myth means we
cannot *really* know or be definite about what we are saying. So,
it is said, in Christian theology, because we use 'mythological'
language to describe the 'beginning' and the 'end', we don't really
know *what happened* at the beginning, nor can we know what will
happen at the end. Indeed, because we have to use 'mythological'
language about the end, as is obviously being done in the book
of Revelation, some wonder whether anything at all will happen
at the end!

We have to be careful. We do have to use 'picture language'
(that is less misleading than the term 'mythological language') to
talk about the Second Coming, life after death, Heaven and Hell.
But Christians have always been aware of that. So Augustine,
writing on the fact that Christians believe that 'Christ is seated
at God's right hand,' says of 'sitting': 'the expression indicates
not a posture of the members, but judicial power, which the
majesty never fails to possess.'[4] Although he did not call this
'mythological' – the word or its equivalent wouldn't have
occurred to him – he knew that this was the way language
worked.

Pre-Copernican myths?

Augustine would never, however, have been doubtful about what
Christ was doing now. He would never have dreamt of saying he
didn't know. For he knew that Christ *was* 'sitting at the right
hand of God'. True, the only way he could talk was to use the
'picture language' that he got from the Bible. But this language
was positive and definite.

The fact that we talk about the future and life after death in
'mythological' terms is irrelevant as far as *reality* is concerned.
The reality of the situations or events we are talking about is not

affected by the kind of language we use. It is vital to remember this. We have, therefore, no need to be hesitant about what we are saying. Of course, we need to be humble and realise that although we see and are not in the dark, we may only be seeing partially. But partial seeing *is* seeing something.

To be hesitant about what we say when we have to use 'picture language' or 'mythological language' is something like this: I ask you, 'What happens at dawn?' And you answer, 'I don't know; all I can do is to use a pre-Copernican myth and say "the sun rises".'

Now, if you say that, I don't think you are clever, but simply incapable of using language. *What* happens in the morning is that the sun *does* rise, as we all know. There is an objective event that happens. We may think that the pre-Copernican myth can be misunderstood. Today we say that the earth goes round the sun and not vice-versa. But as we all know the 'myth' is usually capable of communicating. We can work with it perfectly well. In fact, granted our limitations, namely that we are on earth and not out in space, this is a clear way of talking, clearer than if we had given an answer in post-Copernican scientific terms.

We can now begin to see why to scorn the *descent* of Jesus to the dead as mythological is unreasonable. In the same way we shall see that similar criticism of the Ascension is unreasonable. 'All this belongs to the world of the three-decker universe,' some say. 'Christians and their creeds are tied to this universe. We've rejected such a view of the universe; let's reject these creeds.'

But it is not so simple. The earliest Christians were far less 'spatially' hide bound than we imagine. In any case, they had to, as we have to, use spatial metaphors. This was almost whether they liked it or not. Space goes with value. We normally use metaphors of space to indicate value or superior or inferior position even when there is no question of 'geographical location'. We say, 'Prices are up and wages are down.' In an Examination or Election one person comes out 'on top'; others, in terms of results, are 'underneath' or 'below' or even 'bottom'. So when we say Jesus Christ *descended* to the dead or Hades, we don't mean that he went under the earth. 'The language of descent,' says J. I. Packer, 'is used because Hades, being the place of the disembodied, is *lower* in worth and dignity than life on earth, where body and soul are together and humanity is in that sense whole.'[5]

A second chance?

But why is this doctrine one of hope and assurance? Is it tied in with the idea of a second chance, as some have said?

This clause in the creed has been linked with verses from the first epistle to Peter: 'For Christ also died for sins once for all, the righteous for the unrighteous, that he might bring us to God, being put to death in the flesh but made alive in the spirit; in which he went and preached to the spirits in prison, who formerly did not obey, when God's patience waited in the days of Noah' (1 Pet. 3.18–20).

From these verses it has been felt that there is a basis for hope that after death we can respond to Christ even if in this life we have rejected him. But we need to be cautious.

These verses are very obscure. They were probably less obscure in the time they were written. 'Here we step into a whole world of Jewish mythology which is foreign to most modern readers,' says R. T. France. He is referring to the fascination the sin of the 'sons of God' mentioned in Genesis 6.1–4 had for the Jews in the intertestamental period. These 'sons of God' were regarded as angelic beings who were cast out of heaven because of this sin and were awaiting their punishment at the judgement day. Meanwhile they continue to exercise an evil influence on earth. You can read about these fallen angels in Jude 6 and 2 Peter 2.4. The fullest account is in the Book of Enoch, a book that New Testament writers possibly were familiar with and a book that gives expression to a whole range of Jewish beliefs current at the time of Jesus. There these beings are described as 'spirits', they are in 'prison' and in chapter 12 Enoch is told to go and pronounce to them their punishment.

So it is argued, these verses in Peter don't refer to Christ evangelising among the dead and giving the dead an opportunity to respond to the gospel. They refer to Christ proclaiming his victory over the devil and evil, a victory Paul emphatically said had happened on the cross. There Jesus Christ 'disarmed the principalities and powers and made a public example of them, triumphing over them' (Col. 2.15). On this interpretation the doctrine of the descent of Jesus is not about a 'second chance'.

Others take 'the spirits in prison' as referring to those who died in the flood. The mention of Noah is not simply because the action of the 'sons of God' is associated with the problems of the world in the time of Noah in Genesis 6. It is because Peter is referring to the *men* of Noah's time. These were classic examples of notorious sinners. But these people had never really had a chance of hearing the gospel of Jesus Christ. These verses therefore give a hint that somehow in God's providence such people are not without the opportunity to respond as a result of the death of Christ. The mechanics of this are not for us to understand. But these verses show that of course God is fair.

But even if this is the right interpretation, which is less likely, it is no evidence for a *second* chance after death. These verses could only be said to be suggesting a chance for people who had *no* chance to hear the gospel of Jesus Christ in their life time. So C. E. B. Cranfield, who favours this second interpretation, says that here is 'a hint within the canon of Scripture that the atoning efficacy of Jesus's death was available to those who died in paganism in the ages before Christ, and also, surely, a hint that those who in subsequent ages have died *without ever having had a real chance* to believe in him are not beyond the reach of his saving power' (italics mine).[6]

The emphasis of the Bible is clear. Our destinies are made or marred in this life. 'Do not be deceived;' writes Paul, 'God is not mocked, for whatever a man sows, that he will also reap. For he who sows to his own flesh will from the flesh reap corruption; but he who sows to the Spirit will from the Spirit reap eternal life' (Gal. 6.7–8). The writer of the epistle to the Hebrews similarly implies that opportunity ends with death: 'it is appointed for men to die once, and after that comes judgment' (Heb. 9.27).

'Just men made perfect'

Where then comes the hope in Jesus descent to the dead? Was it in the fact that the Old Testament believers were brought out of the gloom of the twilight world of Sheol into an experience of hope themselves? Is this what the descent achieved? We have seen already that in Old Testament times hope was dim. But the epistle to the Hebrews says Christians 'have come . . . to the assembly of the first-born who are enrolled in heaven, and to a judge who is God of all, and *to the spirits of just men made perfect*' (Heb. 12.23). Is the 'perfecting' being given a new hope, as some have suggested? This is a possibility. The writer of this epistle, after he had catalogued a great list of Old Testament and pre-Christian saints or 'just men', says this: 'all these, though well attested by their faith, did not receive what was promised, since God had forseen something better for us, that apart from us they should not be made perfect' (Heb. 11.39–40). The context of Hebrews shows that Christ is the completer or 'perfecter' (Heb. 12.2) of the Old Testament faith and hope. With the death and resurrection of Christ something has happened to these Old Testament believers – they too have hope.

If this is so, how did this idea come about? Are there any hints of it elsewhere in the New Testament? Some have said that we ought to look at Matthew 27.51–3 in this connection.

These are very odd verses in Matthew's account of the Crucifixion that most commentators gloss over. They read as follows: 'And behold, the curtain of the temple was torn in two, from the top to bottom; and the earth shook, and the rocks were split; and the tombs also were opened, and many bodies of the saints who had fallen asleep were raised, and coming out of the tombs after his resurrection they went into the holy city and appeared to many.'

Reactions to this by commentators are varied. 'The statement of vs 51b–53 (made only by Matthew) is mysterious'[7] is how one commentator puts it. Another one, more sceptical, says: 'We seem to have here a tradition with a legendary element in it.'[8]

What are we to make of this section of Matthew? It is certainly the case that the truth of the resurrection of Jesus doesn't hinge on these verses. Many, therefore, feel it is simplest to say it is a legendary element. But on reflection there are problems about doing this.

'Coming out of the tombs'

First, when we compare this short narrative with examples of contemporary or subsequent legends on the same sort of theme there is a world of difference.

Take a pagan equivalent, the Roman poet Ovid, who knows he is writing legend, the legend of Jason and Medea. This is what real legend is like: 'Then he took the serpent's teeth from the brazen helmet and scattered them over the land he had ploughed. These seeds, which had been steeped before hand in a virulent poison, softened when planted in the ground: as they grew, the teeth that had been sown took on new forms. Just as a baby acquires human shape in its mother's womb, and has all its parts perfectly formed inside her body, only emerging into the light of day when it is complete, so there rose up from the soil, in teeming abundance, a crop of human bodies which had been perfected in the womb of the pregnant earth. More surprising still, they emerged brandishing weapons produced at the same time as themselves.'[9] By comparison Matthew's account of human resurrection is very restrained. But one commentator tells us that Matthew and Ovid are to be compared!

Secondly, there was, it seems, an expectation in Jewish thinking that the resurrection of the dead would take place at Jerusalem when the Mount of Olives would split in two; out of the parting the dead were to appear. But if Matthew or his source wanted to make up an incident to fit in with Jewish expectations, why did he not make it explicit that it happened at the Mount of Olives? It wasn't even a mountain, it is said, that opened but tombs.

Thirdly, it has to be admitted that something happened *physically* at the time of the Crucifixion. The 'veil of the temple' that separated off the 'holy of holies' was torn in two, according to all three synoptic gospels. If it is true, and we have no reason to doubt it, probably the source of this information was the priests who were converted after Pentecost. We have indeed external witness to *something* happening at the Temple. Josephus tells of portents that preceded the fall of Jerusalem (AD 70) and in the Talmud we can read of something happening at a Passover about forty years before the overthrow of the city. 'These statements point to a recollection of *something* extraordinary having taken place in the Temple at the time of the Crucifixion.'[10]

But if we admit the torn veil, did an earthquake take place at the same time? Only Matthew records that. However, there is something interesting in Mark. He tells us that when Jesus died the centurion at the cross exclaimed: 'truly this man was the Son of God!' (Mark 15.39). What made him do that? Would 'a loud cry' as Jesus breathed his last by itself convince him? What Jesus said on the cross may have convinced the centurion that he was innocent as Luke tells us (Luke 23.47). Something more was needed to convince him that he was 'the Son of God', which presumably to him· meant a 'supernatural' person. Something like an earthquake would explain his conviction. Remember, the centurion would have had no knowledge at the time of the veil of the temple being torn. An earthquake would explain the torn veil too! Why should we therefore doubt Matthew over the earthquake?

What then about the opening of the tombs, which he also alone of the Gospel writers mentions? He obviously believed it. Can we – or is it a legend? But if it was, what gave rise to it?

Here is a fourth problem. It is easy to see how the legends that were *based* on these verses took shape. It is not so easy to see how these verses took shape in the first place. A most interesting legend based on these verses is to be found in the apocryphal *Acts of Pilate*.[11] We are told there that the 'saints' raised and then 'appearing' included old Simeon, who had witnessed the presentation of Jesus as a baby in the Temple, and his two sons. Joseph of Arimathea, we are told, took the chief priests to have a chat with them, who in turn wanted Simeon and his sons to give a full account of their experiences of the after life. So they took them back to Jerusalem (they were living out of town), locked them in a synagogue and made them swear to tell the whole truth about their experiences in 'Hades' and their resurrection. They were most obliging and did so. It is fascinating reading. But an obvious fiction.

While we can see how Matthew gives rise to legends, what could give rise to Matthew? Some sort of event! Suppose events of the sort Matthew talks about happened. Would it be very different from the transfiguration, when Old Testament figures

appeared to Peter, James and John? Would it perhaps have something to do with the 'perfecting' of the Old Testament saints.
We can't be certain. Nevertheless we *can* surely say, along with
F. F. Bruce, that in these verses in Matthew 'there is a suggestion
that the death of Christ caused a radical disturbance in the realm
of the dead; his victorious supremacy is attested over the grave,
for "to this end Christ died and lived again, that he might be
Lord both of the dead and of the living" (Rom. 14.9)'.[12]

Practical hope

It has to be admitted that the doctrine of the descent of Christ
to the dead is not one of the essentials of the faith. Indeed it is
not in all the early creeds. It is not in the Nicene Creed, the
creed often recited at Holy Communion services. It is, of course,
in the Apostles' Creed.

Its importance is not so much theological as practical. It is a
doctrine of practical importance for the Christian, and it is here
you get assurance and hope. It tells us that Jesus Christ was truly
and utterly human, as well as divine. He really died. He 'entered
Hades'. He experienced all that death means from a human point
of view.

This is indeed good news. It is a wonderful answer to our
natural fear of death. Even though we may believe that God has
accepted us in Christ, as the Christian believes to be the case,
we can still be worried and anxious in the face of death. No
doubt for some who read these words death may be relatively
near. While you may believe that the 'sting of death' has been
drawn by Christ (1 Cor. 15.56), you may still fear the 'act of
dying'. Like a child going into a darkened room, in their better
moments they know there is nothing to fear. But they still prefer
to go into that room *with* someone else.

The 'descent to the dead' by Jesus tells us that he knows all
about that darkened room of death. What is more by his 'descent'
he seems to have turned that darkened room, which used to be
thought of as a place of 'shadows', truly into a place of pleasure,
'paradise'. At least that is where he promised the penitent thief
he would go that first Good Friday (Luke 23.43). And as we will
soon see, Jesus wants that to be a room without shadows for us.

He wants to go *with* us into and through that room of death when our time comes. He wants to be with us in our dying and our death. The doctrine of the 'descent' tells us that he is an experienced traveller. The Puritans knew that well. Richard Baxter put it like this 300 years ago: 'Christ leads me through no darker room than he went through before'. And John Preston, another Puritan, when he lay dying was asked if he feared death. 'No', he whispered, 'I shall change my place, but I shall not change my company.'[13]

So it makes a difference practically if you understand something of all this. Nor was it only for Puritans for whom it provided assurance and hope. Pope John 23rd, before he died, said, 'My bags are packed – I'm ready to go.' What wonderful Christian confidence. What a contrast with that remark of Bertrand Russell: 'There is darkness without, and when I die there will be darkness within.' That is one of the prices of rejecting Jesus Christ and the hope of the resurrection.

Conclusion

The 'descent' of Jesus is not out-moded mythology; rather it is useful 'picture language'. It does not encourage us to hope for a 'second chance'. It may be connected with the 'perfecting' of Old Testament 'saints', bringing them light and life where before there was darkness. But it certainly can and should give us confidence in the face of death when it confronts us.

11: Where did Jesus go? – 'to prepare a place'

'Don't worry'

The answer that Jesus himself gave to our question 'Where did Jesus go?' was that he was going to 'prepare a place' for his followers (John 14.3). The knowledge of this was to be an antidote to worry, stress and strain.

A soldier who served in the second World War lives in Newcastle upon Tyne in the north of England, where I live. He was a hero in the North Africa campaign under Montgomery. But then his unit was mistakenly shipped to Salerno in Italy. Communication failure followed on communication failure and incompetence followed on incompetence on the part of some of his superiors. He and the men under him had had enough. They were not cowards – they had proved that. But they just sat down and refused to move and refused to fight. Court Martial followed. The soldier was sentenced to death. Had the sentence been carried out it would have been the only one of its kind in the war. Somehow it was suspended – but the disgrace remained.

Forty years later the sentencing officer and the soldier met face to face in a television studio.[1] There were tears in the soldier's eyes. The former officer, now a QC, was asked if he had been right to pronounce the death sentence. 'Yes,' he replied under great stress, 'mutiny is mutiny, whatever the mitigating circumstances.'

So much of life is terribly tangled. Jesus knew this only too well. He knew that life can be very hard, very often, for very many.

We live in a troubled world. None of us are immune from the stresses and strains of life. Jesus himself experienced stress. At times he was extremely *distressed*. People weeping when his friend

Lazarus died was more than he could bear (John 11.33). Thoughts of his own death troubled him (John 12.27) – there was nothing unnatural about Jesus' own response to death. And he was troubled at the knowledge that one of his own group of disciples would betray him (John 13.21). John says he was 'troubled in spirit.'

But Jesus does not want us to be troubled. In his last supper talk with his disciples he said, 'Let not your hearts be troubled' (John 14.1). He didn't want and he doesn't want his followers to be unnecessarily worried. He was reported as saying in the Sermon on the Mount: 'Do not be anxious about tomorrow, for tomorrow will be anxious for itself' (Matt. 6.34).

However, we need to note that Jesus doesn't promise that the future will be trouble free. The world of 'tomorrow' is not seen as an easier world. 'Tomorrow' will not necessarily bring a release from troubles. But these troubles do not have to invade our hearts. But how do you stop them doing so. Norman Vincent Peale tells people to 'put all their cares in the waste-paper basket at the end of the day, just like a man cleaning out all his pockets and throwing into the basket all the unnecessary bits and pieces.'[2] But unless you believe that someone is going to dispose of all the rubbish, it will stay there to haunt you. It is all very well to say, 'Don't worry' or 'Don't be troubled', but how do you stop?

Immediately after Jesus had told his disciples not to let their hearts be troubled, he said: 'Believe in God.' They were to have their eyes fixed on their loving heavenly Father. They needed to know that God was their creator. In the Sermon on the Mount when he was talking about worry, he had argued this point. If God had already put us on this earth, he can look after us. If God watches over the birds and the flowers, of course, he will watch over us (Matt. 6.25–34).

So Jesus said: 'Let not your hearts be troubled; believe in God.'

'I go to prepare a place'

But Jesus says something more is needed. A general belief in the sovereignty of God is good but not enough, if we are to overcome worry and anxiety. Jesus said, according to John, that we need quite specifically to believe in him. 'Believe in God, *believe also in me.*' Why?

The problem for the disciples at the time was that Christ had indicated he would soon die! Their worries had to do with his death. Perhaps some of them thought they might die too. As we have seen they clearly did not understand all Jesus was saying. But talk of death was in the air. Peter had just said that he would be willing to 'lay down his life for Jesus' (John 13.37). So Jesus proceeds to give some teaching on how to face death without the wrong sort of worry.

A consultant surgeon once said to me, 'I don't know what to say to people about to die.' How sad! We have already noted that today many people don't know how to face death. It wasn't so different in the ancient world. Aristotle once said: 'Now death is the most terrible of all things, for it is the end.' The world was a world without hope. But when the Christian gospel of the resurrection from the dead was preached, a new hope came into the ancient world. It was so often 'hope' that marked off the Christians. So when someone from the pagan world wanted to quiz a Christian on what he believed, it was his 'hope' that he wanted to know about. So the early Christians were told to 'be prepared to make a defence to any one who calls you to account for the *hope* that is in you' (1 Pet. 3.15).

Part of this hope, which meant that death could now be faced, came from Jesus telling his disciples where he was going. This was to enable them to face death without worry.

So he says: 'I go to prepare a place for you' (John 14.2). What exactly does that mean?

Well, it certainly speaks of a separation, in the immediate future, of Jesus from his disciples. But the word 'prepare' suggests that their parting will not be for ever. It will only be temporary. Some of his disciples had gone on to 'prepare' the room where Jesus now was having his last supper with the disciples; then the rest had joined them when all was ready. In the same way Jesus has gone on, he seems to say, to prepare a place for his followers. In time they will join him. For this separation implies a reunion.

'So Jesus bids us think of death,' writes John Stott, 'not as a leap into the dark unknown. but as a journey to a prepared place.

It will not be like arriving in a strange town in a foreign land, where you know nobody, nobody is expecting you and you haven't even made a hotel reservation. No. Just as Jesus had sent two of his disciples ahead into the city to prepare for him to eat the passover (Mark 14.12–15), so now he would go ahead to prepare for them.'[3]

Did Jesus say anything more about where he was going? Yes. He was specific. He spoke of 'the place' as being 'in my Father's house' where there 'are many rooms' (John 14.2). What were these 'many rooms'? Probably the reference is to 'lodging places' where travellers in New Testament times could find rest and security at night. So Jesus is suggesting that he is going to a place of rest and security, and such a place awaits us the other side of death! And there is a lot of space there. There are 'many rooms'. The Bible, far from suggesting that heaven is only to be peopled by a tiny remnant, says that it will be peopled by 'a great multitude which no man could number, from every nation, from all tribes and peoples and tongues' (Rev. 7.9).

Jesus did not only say he was going 'to prepare a place'. He then said, 'when I go and prepare a place for you, I will come again and will take you to myself, that where I am you may be also' (John 14.3). He has gone on but promises to come back. And he will come back, in person, and then take us with him. We won't have to go it alone. He will be by our side. This is what he seems to be saying.

When will this be? The first answer is, 'at his second coming.' But surely this promise can also be seen to apply to our own deaths. It can be said that at that time Christ comes to take us to himself. And where exactly will we go? To be with Christ. 'I will take you to myself.' 'Christ is to be our destination as well as our escort. *He* comes to take us, and he takes us to *himself*.'[4]

Life after death

Who wants to know what is the essential New Testament teaching about the future life? Here it is! If you are a Christian and you want to know about your final state after the resurrection at the last day, the answer is here. If you are a Christian and want to know about the 'intermediate' state, the state between death and the resurrection, the answer is here. Both states are spoken of as being 'with Christ' or 'with the Lord', for Jesus takes us to himself.

This was Paul's teaching. When he was speaking of the intermediate state as he saw it, he said that he had a 'desire to depart and be *with* Christ, for that is far better' (Phil. 1.23). But then he spoke of the final state in these words, 'so we shall always be *with* the Lord' (1 Thess. 4.17). That is the main thing we need to know.

There is a story told of a doctor visiting a patient's home. He used to take his dog around with him. He left the dog downstairs on this visit. Upstairs was a man who was dying.

'What is heaven like?' asked the man. 'I don't know,' replied the doctor who happened to be a convinced Christian. But at that moment he heard his dog scratching at the door of the patient's room. It gave him an idea. 'Can you hear my dog?' 'Yes.' 'He has no idea what is in this room. He has simply heard my voice and come up the stairs to find me. He knows I am here and wants to find me.' He went on, 'Heaven perhaps is like that. Jesus is there but we don't know what is inside the room! My dog wants to come in here because I am here. Similarly we can look forward to going to heaven, because Jesus is there.'[5]

We can know *something* of heaven. There will be full personal existence. The empty tomb is a denial of some 'shadowy soul survival'. There will be a true resurrection of which Christ is the 'firstfruits'.

We know *enough* about heaven. We no longer have to live with doubts and uncertainties like the believers in Old Testament times, for Christ not only 'abolished death', he has 'brought life and immortality *to light* through the gospel' (2 Tim. 1.10). As Murray Harris writes: 'only with the death and resurrection of Christ did the ideas of resurrection and immortality emerge from Old Testament shadows into the full light of New Testament day.'[6]

That is why meditating on the resurrection of Jesus and all that goes with it is a comfort in death. When Paul himself was in prison and facing the prospect of death, it was the resurrection of Jesus that was one of the things uppermost in his mind. In the Pastoral epistles to Timothy we have what looks like Paul's last thoughts; and in the second epistle Timothy is told to 'Remember Jesus Christ, risen from the dead' (2 Tim. 2.8). Paul was aware that, as he said, 'the time of my departure has come' (2 Tim. 4.6). He knew he was soon to die. But Christ's resurrection gave him hope.

Paul

How did Paul think that the resurrection of Jesus affected life beyond the grave? Can we fill out his thinking?

Before his conversion Paul would have followed one of the traditions of the Pharisees about life after death. Some of them certainly believed 'that there will be a resurrection of both the just and the unjust' (Acts 24.15). Many at the time believed this. Martha did. She said of her dead brother, 'I know he will rise again in the resurrection at the last day' (John 11.24). This is most likely to have been Paul's pre-conversion position. Paul didn't, therefore, need to change his views on this. But of course the 'new thing' was that Paul, after his conversion, believed that in Jesus the resurrection *had begun*. Resurrection was now more than a hope; it was a fact. And since God had raised Jesus, he would certainly raise his people one day.

There were those who had died before the second coming of Christ, his *parousia* – to use the Greek word. These, Paul teaches, will be 'raised' before that event and Christ will bring them with him. 'For since we believe that Jesus died and rose again, even so, through Jesus, God will bring with him those who have fallen asleep' (1 Thess. 4.14). (Note: they are asleep 'with him').

But what about those who are still alive when Christ comes again? They won't need to be 'raised', says Paul. No. They will need to be 'changed'. Nor will it need to be a total transformation, because in some way the resurrection principle is at work in them now. Their bodies indeed have the *new life* principle working in them now because they have been united with Christ through faith. The spirit of Christ is at work in them. In baptism the Christian has been buried with Christ, 'so that as Christ was raised from the dead by the glory of the Father, we too might walk in newness of life. For if we have been united with him in a death like his, we shall certainly be united with him in a resurrection like his' (Rom. 6.4–5). The same argument also comes later in the epistle to the Romans: 'If the Spirit of him who raised Jesus from the dead dwells in you, he who raised Christ Jesus from the dead will give life to your mortal bodies also through his Spirit which dwells in you' (Rom. 8.11).

But when Christ comes there will be an immediate transformation to complete this process and to ensure that those who survive will be adapted to the conditions of the new age which then will have fully come. 'We shall not all sleep, but we shall all be changed, in a moment, in the twinkling of an eye, at the last trumpet. For the trumpet will sound, and the dead will be raised imperishable, and we shall be changed' (1 Cor. 15.51–2). This is in line with what he said to his friends at Philippi: 'the Lord Jesus Christ . . . will change our lowly body to be like his glorious body, by the power which enables him even to subject all things to himself' (Phil. 3.21).

This body, according to Paul, is called a 'spiritual' body (Greek: *sōma pneumatikon*). The present body is called a 'natural' or 'physical' (RSV) body (Greek: *sōma psychikon*). 'Spiritual' has the Old Testament sense, not of 'immaterial', but of 'belonging to the life of God'. 'Natural' or 'physical' means not 'material', but 'belonging to the life of this world'. The relationship between the two was hinted at by means of the analogy of the seed and the ripe grain: 'it is sown a physical body, it is raised a spiritual body' (1 Cor. 15.44).

Can we really believe this? Can we today really believe there will be the sound of the trumpet?

Of course, this is 'picture language' again. The 'parousia' was a special term used in the first century to describe an official visit by the emperor or by a king. It was a 'royal visit'. There was 'pomp and circumstance' and special shouts as well as the noise of the crowds. There were trumpets blown and no doubt all sorts of other noises. This was, perhaps, the best picture Paul could think up for the coming of the one before whom one day 'every knee would bow' (Phil. 2.10). Of course, he knew that the 'coming' of *this* 'king' would be of an altogether different order to that of a state visit in the Graeco-Roman world. But the picture would have been easily understood.

Dying

What did Paul actually think happened at death? At first he no doubt thought that he himself would be one of those to be 'changed'. He would be alive when Christ returned. As Christ had made it clear that no one could know the date of his return, it has always been a Christian instinct to live in 'readiness' for that return. It *might* be tomorrow! But as time went on and Paul was suffering more and more for his faith, he realised that death might come to him *before* Christ returned.

We have Paul's views on dying in the second epistle to the Corinthians. 'We know that if the earthly tent we live in is destroyed, we have a building from God, a house not made with hands, eternal in the heavens. Here indeed we groan, and long to put on our heavenly dwelling, so that by putting it on we may not be found naked. For while we are still in this tent, we sigh with anxiety; not that we would be unclothed, but that we would be further clothed, so that what is mortal may be swallowed up by life. He who has prepared us for this very thing is God, who has given us the Spirit as a guarantee' (2 Cor. 5.1–5).

Immediately after death the fact and the consciousness is one of being with Jesus. Jesus said to the dying thief who was penitent, 'today you will be with me in Paradise' (Luke 23.43). There will not, says Paul, be a state of being 'unclothed, but of being further clothed' – that will be the experience at death. Is this different to what Paul had said in his first epistle to the Corinthians? *There* he said the resurrection of the believer took place in association with the second coming of Christ. This was in line with Jesus' teaching recorded in John: 'the hour is coming when all who are in the tombs will hear his voice and come forth, those who have done good, to the resurrection of life, and those who have done evil, to the resurrection of judgment' (John 5.28–9).

Perhaps the clue is that Paul is talking in 2 Corinthians about the *experience* or *consciousness* of the individual at death. That is to say, in the consciousness of the believer at death there is no interval between bodily dissolution and the renewed body – the mortal being 'swallowed up by life'. But the interval measured by the calendar of secular history may require a longer timescale. This fits in with Pauls use of the word 'sleep' to describe those who 'rest in the Lord'. 'Sleep is essentially timeless,' writes C. K. Barrett. 'Between the moment of falling asleep and that of waking five minutes or five hours by the clock may intervene, but the sleeper himself passes instantaneously from one to the other.'[7] Or perhaps that is too easy a solution to what is an inscrutable mystery.

Be that as it may, Paul certainly believed that to 'depart and be with Christ' was *far better*. It was far better than continuing to live on in the plain of earth bound history, however necessary it was for him to do that (Phil. 1.23).

It is very hard for many people to imagine someone really looking forward to death. But Paul did and he didn't do it in a morbid way. We can see that from the second letter to Timothy; there we have Paul's own self disclosure as he faces death. It is a wonderful passage. I can remember once hearing it read at a most moving funeral service that I attended.

It was a funeral of a young man. He'd been travelling in his car on the A1 in the North-East of England, when a lorry coming in the opposite direction burst a tyre, crashed into him and took his car right off the road. He was killed.

At the funeral service, his wife, who was only in her twenties, spoke for a few minutes in the place of the sermon. She just said that before her husband died, he'd been preparing his lesson for his Pathfinder Bible class for the following Sunday. He never gave the lesson. But he left notes; and the Bible lesson he was to give came from this very passage of Paul, 2 Timothy 4.7-8. These were the verses open on his desk: 'I have fought the good fight, I have finished the race, I have kept the faith, henceforth there is laid up for me the crown of righteousness which the Lord, the righteous judge will award to me on that Day.' That young girl believed that was true for her husband as well as for Paul. She knew that Christ has 'abolished death' through the gospel of the Resurrection.

The only way

So we can see that Paul is not contradicting anything said or implied by Jesus in his last supper discourse in John 14 about life beyond the grave. Indeed Paul claims in one place that his teaching on these matters has come ultimately not from a special revelation from God to himself but from what he has learnt from Jesus own teaching: 'For this we declare to you by the word of the Lord . . .' (1 Thess. 4.15).

But one thing we have not so far noted about Jesus teaching in John 14 is this: he says that we can only really understand all he has to say in answer to our question 'Where did Jesus go?' when we realise that he is the only way to God. When Thomas said to Jesus, ' "Lord, we do not know where you are going; how can we know the way?" Jesus said to him, "I am the way, and the truth, and the life; no one comes to the Father, but by me" ' (John 14.5–6).

This is an uncomfortable statement for many today. 'Don't all ways lead to God? Aren't all the religions of the world like the flowers in a garden? They are all beautiful flowers in their own ways. *Together* they complement each other and set each other off. We need them all.' A Muslim once told me this is how he saw things; the world of religions was like a garden.

However, there was something exclusive about the claims of Jesus Christ. But were these justified?

Was he so special? More particularly was the Resurrection so unique anyway? Isn't resurrection common to a number of the world's religions? What is the answer?

It depends on what you mean by 'resurrection'. The answer is definitely 'No, not at all,' if we are talking about the resurrection of a *man in history* who left an actual grave.

It is this historical element that marks off Christianity from the other religions. All religions tell us something of what is believed to be God's *nature*. But Christianity tells us that at a certain time and in a certain place God has *acted* in a decisive way. The essence of Christianity is not so much its teaching about God, but the event God caused to happen – the birth, death and resurrection of Jesus Christ. History is so central. This is so different, for example, to Hinduism, where there is more of a concern with ideas than with history. A missionary bishop, Lesslie Newbigin, tells us about a meeting he had with one of the teachers of the Rāmankrishnan Mission. This man couldn't believe that the Bishop was willing to rest his whole faith as a Christian upon the basic historical truth of the New Testament account of what Jesus said and did. 'To him it seemed axiomatic that such vital matters of religious truth could not be allowed to depend upon the accidents of history.'[8] He would certainly not want them to depend on the fact of the resurrection of a man in history.

For parallels to the Resurrection we can begin with the religions of the Ancient Near East. Think back to that Arab peasant working just off the Syrian coast at the eastern end of the Mediterranean in 1928. He struck a slab of stone and discovered the ancient remains and civilisation of Ugarit from the second millenium BC. Soon Dr C. F. A. Schaeffer and his team of French archaeologists were to dig some tablets from the soil where they had been hidden for 3,500 years.

They appeared to contain stories of a dying and rising god, Baal – the Canaanite God – that we read about in the pages of the Old Testament. After his victories over various enemies, we can read in the tablets of how eventually he dies and goes to the underworld of the God Mot (death). He stays there for a period, but then seems to come back to life in the upper world with a little help from Shapesh (the Sun Goddess).

Half the words on the tablets are missing or undecipherable.[9] No one really knows for sure the details of the myth of Baal. Perhaps this was supposed to be seen as a 'mythical' death and resurrection. If so, it is most definitely not something on the plain of history; we are dealing with (mythical) gods, and not men.

Then there was Tammuz. He is referred to in the Old Testament in the book of Ezekiel. The prophet saw women in the North Gate of the Temple in Jerusalem 'weeping for Tammuz' (Ezek. 8.14). Who was he? He features in the Babylonian *Epic of Gilgamesh*, a blood thirsty saga, if ever.[10] The myth tells us that when Tammuz died, his wife, the Goddess Ishtar, followed him to the underworld to try to rescue him. In the story he may have experienced resurrection. However, some scholars think he didn't. If he did, it was just for half a year. Or was it simply that his ghost came back – that is another possibility? Whatever the right interpretation, we are again dealing with the 'gods'. We are not talking about dateable history.

The mystery religions

In New Testament times there was the cult of Isis. This was one of the so called 'mystery religions' and very popular around the Mediterranean world in those days. Isis was originally an Egyptian goddess. Her husband Osiris was murdered brutally by his brother Seth. All was not lost, however, as he managed to become king of the dead. He therefore had a new life, but *in the underworld*. We wouldn't consider that much of a resurrection! In any case the way Isis reassembled thirteen of the fourteen pieces into which Osiris corpse had been dismembered and then magically resuscitated them is hardly a parallel with the New Testament account of the resurrection of Jesus!

Then there were the Isis cult rites themselves. It is true you have the theme of death and resurrection there. A rather bawdy second century AD story-teller, Apuleius, tells us that the theme is found in the initiation rites. In his *Golden Ass* we read that the initiate into the mysteries of Isis 'approaches the very gate of death' and yet is 'permitted to return.'[11]

Something happened like this in the mysteries of Mithras – a god the Roman soldiers seemed to have liked. But again, as in the rites of Isis, death and resurrection is only 'symbolic'. It was a symbolic death and resurrection that the initiate went through. Who could confuse the symbolic rebirth into one of the grades of the cult with the resurrection of Jesus? We are not comparing like with like.

There was another mystery cult where devotion was paid to Attis. Attis was a vegetation god from Asia Minor and the lover of Cybele, the great Earth Mother. In the story of the myth he dies and comes to life again. But the evidence for this is late – from the second century AD; so the cult myth could easily have been influenced by the Christian belief in the resurrection of Christ. The 'mysteries' were quite 'syncretistic'; they took on board all sorts of ideas that were fashionable. Anyhow, as J. N. D. Anderson writes: 'There is all the difference in the world between the rising and re-birth of a deity which symbolises the coming of spring (and the reawakening of nature) and the resurrection "on the third day" of an historical person.'[12]

The mystery religions popular at the time of the rise of Christianity were religious responses to the break up of the old traditional Roman religion and the traditional way of life. Perhaps they were something like the 'cults' in the modern Western world. It was *joining* that was most important with the companionship that followed. 'Beliefs' were not important. So whether the gods really 'rose' was not an issue. In fact you could be in a number of mystery cults at the same time.

Someone says, 'let's leave the twilight world of the mystery religions. What about the more established religions of today? What about Islam? If Hinduism is not an historical religion, Islam surely is. Can't we find an historical resurrection there?' No.

When Muhammad had literally just breathed his last and died, Omar, we are told, rushed out of the tent with his sabre drawn. He threatened to strike off the head of anyone who dared say the prophet was no more. He hoped for 'continued life' for his leader. That is the nearest you get to resurrection!

Of course, Muhammad's followers never seriously claimed that the prophet lived on without dying. They certainly never made the claim that he rose from the dead. In fact when the devout Muslim fulfils the fifth of his religious duties and makes the pilgrimage to Mecca, what does he often do? He visits the mosque at al-Madīna where the prophet was buried in the hut of his wife.

Nor is there a claim for resurrection for other historical figures in the world's main religions or secular philosophies. James Orr put it like this: 'There is no instance in history, apart from Christianity, of a religion established on the belief in the resurrection of its founder.'[13] David Watson says this: 'The tomb of Lenin is one of the show pieces in Russia. And it is *not* an empty tomb . . . The bones of Lenin are in Moscow. The bones of Muhammad are in Medina. The bones of Buddha are in India. But in Jerusalem is the empty tomb.'[14]

Conclusion

Jesus tells his disciples that he is going 'to prepare a place' for them, to help them not to worry about death. If he does not first return, he will take them through death to life with himself. But

there is only one way to God and to 'resurrection life' – through
Jesus Christ, who lived in history, died and rose again.

12: Where did Jesus go? – 'to the right hand of God'

It's the asides that matter

Towards the end of his life the distinguished BBC anchor man and broadcaster, Richard Dimbleby, was in Germany covering a visit of Queen Elizabeth to the Berlin Wall. All had been set up for a live commentary. Transmission was due to begin. But then all communication with London seemed to be lost and Dimbleby lost his proverbial poise. He lost his temper. There was a red-hot argument over this technical disaster.

The trouble was everything said was actually being transmitted and being received perfectly well in London! Richard Dimbleby wasn't aware. All could be heard – the language, the lot! For once people had a glimpse of someone other than the smooth and utterly polite English gentleman that was Richard Dimbleby's usual TV image. Here instead was someone under pressure, with high standards, who could not tolerate sloppiness and was provoked by seeming inefficiency. It was not the commentary but the asides that showed all this. They showed the man behind the image.

When you come to study the Bible it is very much the same. It is not just the central and more obvious statements that are important. So often it is the asides. These show us what the writers really thought and believed when, if you like, they were off their guard. Take the section from Peter's first epistle we have already referred to, where he speaks of Christ going and preaching to 'the spirits in prison'. He then mentions Noah's ark and the Flood, which leads him on to say: 'Baptism which corresponds to this, now saves you, not as a removal of dirt from the body but as an appeal to God for a clear conscience, through the resurrection of Jesus Christ, who has gone into heaven and is at the right hand of God, with angels, authorities, and powers subject to him' (1 Pet. 3.21–2).

Much of this is almost as obscure as the question of the 'descent' to the 'spirits in prison'. For example how are we to think of baptism? Christians have been divided over this question and it still continues to exercise them. But those controversial issues mustn't make us ignore the little verse tucked in at the end. We can easily overlook it.

Here Peter is talking about the resurrection of Jesus Christ and says that this means he 'has gone into heaven and is at the right hand of God, with angels, authorities, and powers subject to him.' This is just an aside, but it is of supreme significance. For *if you had asked someone in the Apostolic age, 'Where did Jesus go?', this is probably the answer you would have been given: 'He has gone into heaven and is at the right hand of God.'*

This is significant because it shows us how Peter viewed Jesus at the time he was writing. This was the Jesus of his present experience. It shows us what the New Testament Christians actually believed about Jesus even when they faced terrible problems including persecution. For Peter is writing to Christians under threat of persecution. And what it shows is this: from all the different things that could be said about the risen Jesus, one thing stood out above the rest and of this they were sure – Jesus was *exalted*; he was and is over all; or as Paul put it, 'he is the beginning, the first-born from the dead, that in everything he might be pre-eminent' (Col. 1.18).

Peter's words, however, are not a studied theological statement. It is an almost unconscious remark. He can't help saying this. For this is the Jesus he knows now. He is not just the risen Christ but the *ascended* Christ. As an eyewitness to the Ascension, as Luke reports, he had seen something that convinced him, if he didn't know already, that Jesus was 'at the right hand of God, with angels, authorities, and powers subject to him.' Peter had further experienced this on the day of Pentecost. That was when the ascended Christ released the Holy Spirit in a remarkable way for the Church. As Jesus had earlier promised, the disciples would be 'clothed with power from on high' (Luke 24.49). Because this had happened Peter and the other Apostles were able to defy the hostile Jewish authorities and proclaim 'in Jesus the resurrection from the dead' (Acts 4.2).

We may find this hard to understand. Peter didn't. He knew something first hand of the victory of Christ and the fact that he was King. He believed that something was now true in the universe of space and time and beyond. That is why he could give a message of hope to his readers. Maybe they were, or some were, in terrible suffering. Some were, when he was writing, being persecuted for their faith in Jesus Christ. But this would only be for a short time, because, as a straightforward matter of fact, Christ was the victor and reigning and in control. He'd personally experienced that in a dramatic way on one occasion, according to Acts, when he was freed from prison (Acts 12.3–11). True, at the very same time Herod had 'killed James the brother of John with the sword' (Acts 12.2). There is a mystery in suffering. It is seldom easy to understand. But what Peter would say is this: the last word is not with suffering but with Christ.

This is the message of the book of Revelation, where Jesus is portrayed not only as the 'Lamb' who was sacrificed, but also the 'Lamb at the throne'. So the cry 'of many angels, numbering myriads of myriads and thousands of thousands' is this: 'Worthy is the Lamb who was slain, to receive power and wealth and wisdom and might and honour and glory and blessing!' (Rev. 5.11–12).

'Jesus Christ, who has gone into heaven'

It is amazing how hazy people can be over the ascension of Jesus Christ. Once I was talking to a younger person, who was very well educated. 'Yes,' he said, 'I believe in the Ascension; but I don't believe in the resurrection of Jesus'!

Taken at its face value the New Testament seems to be relatively clear. The main evidence is in Luke and Acts.

Easter in Jerusalem had gone – that was the period of the Passover and the few days of unleavened bread. As we have said, many of the disciples who were predominantly from Galilee in the North must have returned home. The distance was short. Some weeks later it was time to visit Jerusalem again for the Festival of Pentecost, or the 'feast of weeks'. So back they went;

and in Jerusalem they had a final encounter with the risen Jesus. He gave them a charge: this time they were to stay in Jerusalem and to wait for the coming of the promised Holy Spirit.

And then in Acts 1.9 we read this: 'When he had said this, as they were looking on, he was lifted up, and a cloud took him out of their sight.'

Many people today find that impossible to believe. Yes, they can theoretically cope, just about, with the idea of 'miracle'; and then when they have looked at the evidence, they have to admit that something happened that first Easter. But the Ascension – that is too much to be asked to believe.

John Robinson was a Bishop of Woolwich in the nineteen sixties and wrote the book *Honest to God*. In it he popularised the radical theology that, arguably, has lead to the loss of nerve and vitality in the Church in England. But what for us is interesting is that he begins the book with some remarks on the Ascension: 'Even such an educated man of the world as St Luke can express the conviction of Christ's ascension – the conviction that he is not merely alive but reigns in the might and right of God – in the crudest terms of being 'lifted up' into heaven, there to sit down at the right hand of the Most High.'[1]

In a similar vein C. J. Cadoux had written earlier about the body of Jesus rising 'vertically off the surface of the earth' and disappearing into the sky: 'Such an occurrence is so hard to believe, that nothing save the most unimpeachable evidence could justify one in believing it . . . It is much simpler and more satisfying to abandon altogether the idea of an ascension of Jesus' body and to regard the belief in such an ascension and Luke's description of it as resulting naturally from the need of explaining why the series of visions came to an end.'[2] But, 'Why,' asks G. R. Beasley-Murray, 'discredit Luke's reliability at this point?'[3]

Cosmology

Again we have the problem of the 'three decker universe' or so we are told. Modern science has changed our understanding of the physical universe. Previously it was alright to talk of 'heaven above'. In those days people could cope with the Ascension. But we can't today.

Is that true? We have already talked about the need for 'spatial' metaphors which the New Testament writers needed as much as we need them today. It is by no means certain that they were talking 'primitive cosmology' when they talked about the ascension of Jesus or were implying a *belief* in a primitive world view.

There has been a Christian instinct never to put absolute confidence in any cosmological system or scientific theory about the nature of the physical universe. 'Natural scientists and philosophers have attempted to explain "nature"; but not one of their theories or systems has remained firm and unshaken; but each is overthrown by its successor.' And this was not said at the time of the nineteenth century controversies over Science and Religion, nor even at the time of Galileo. It came from the pen of Basil of Cappodocia in the fourth century AD in his *Hexaëmeron*.[4]

What is so noticeable about the New Testament is the absence of reference to the structure of the universe of space. In the Jewish intertestamental literature as indeed in Gnostic literature this often seems to be a preoccupation. In *2 Enoch*, for example, we are given a veritable 'hitch-hiker's guide to the galaxy', as Enoch goes not only through the 'seven heavens' but on to the 'tenth' to meet God and get his secrets; and these included the secrets of how the universe was made and formed. But in the Book of Revelation there is hardly any 'cosmological geography'. At the end of the seven letters to the churches (including Smyrna) we read this: 'After this I looked, and lo, in heaven an open door! And the first voice, which I had heard speaking to me like a trumpet, said, "Come up hither, and I will show you what must take place after this." *At once* I was in the Spirit, and lo, a throne stood in heaven, with one seated on the throne!' (Rev. 4.1–2). Heaven is 'up'; but there is no 'journey' there. 'At once' he is there 'in the Spirit'. There is no flying through the various 'heavens'. The language of the 'three decker' universe was certainly used in Revelation as elsewhere but it is figurative.

Paul spoke of being 'caught up to the third heaven', the location of 'Paradise', when he was describing a visionary experience (2 Cor. 12.2–3). But this is not a *journey* to another place in a distant part of the universe; rather, in Paul, it reads like a translation to a different *order* of existence. By the time he is writing the 'third heaven' is probably a synonym for 'Paradise'. That is where it was traditionally located. It was therefore a figure of speech. Indeed speculation on these cosmological questions was discouraged by Paul. People were not 'to occupy themselves with myths and endless genealogies' – Jewish and Gnostic speculations based on the Old Testament creation story (1 Tim. 1.4).

We mustn't assume that the New Testament writers were naïve, nor that people before our time were naïve in these matters – 'as people of limited intelligence are fond of doing' (Tolstoy describing Vera Berg in *War and Peace* when she spoke of 'our days' in a superior way). People have had queries and questions about the Ascension long before the rise of modern science. Before the Reformation you can find scribal comments on early manuscripts about the problem of the Ascension. One scribe once suggested that if anyone was stupid enough to think of Christ as travelling through space, assuming a pre-Copernican view, it would take an enormous length of time for Christ even to reach the first heaven, let alone the seventh! There have been sensitive Christians aware of the issues throughout the centuries.

The meaning of the Ascension

What was the relationship between the Resurrection and the Ascension? We need to remind ourselves that the resurrection of Jesus was not a resuscitation to normal earthly life. It was the beginning of the new age, the first-fruits of that new kingdom. 'The resurrection of Jesus was the emergence of eternal life in the midst of mortality.'[5] In this context some see the resurrection and 'exaltation' of Jesus – his being raised to the right of God – as one.

Peter links the two in his Pentecost sermon: 'This Jesus God raised up, and of that we all are witnesses. Being *therefore* exalted at the right hand of God . . .' (Acts 2.32–3). Also in the early hymn that seems to lie behind Philippians 2 you have the death of Jesus followed by his exaltation, with no resurrection in between: 'being found in human form he humbled himself and became obedient to death, even death on a cross. Therefore God has highly exalted him and bestowed on him the name which is above every name, that at the name of Jesus every knee should bow, in heaven and on earth and under the earth, and every tongue confess that Jesus Christ is Lord, to the glory of God the Father' (Phil 2.8–11). It is possible, therefore, that the early Christians saw the resurrection and exaltation of Jesus all as one. But if that is so, if they are intimately linked, is that a reason for dismissing Luke's account as really an intrusion?

Michael Ramsey, the former Archbishop of Canterbury, says 'No!': 'The tradition in Luke concerning the Ascension as a distinct event cannot be dismissed. There is nothing incredible in an event whereby Jesus assured the disciples that the appearances were ended and that his sovereignty and his presence must henceforth be sought in new ways.'[6]

There is obviously something profound about the Ascension; it is a profound mystery. But whatever we might feel unable to say about it, it was certainly, as Luke shows us, a *final* event. It was the last of the appearances of Christ to his disciples. It was the signal that the end of Jesus' resurrection appearances had come. Only once after this did he appear again, and that, as we have already seen, was said to be highly irregular: 'Last of all, as to one untimely born, he appeared also to me,' wrote Paul (1 Cor. 15.8). Paul knew that his seeing the risen Christ was outside the main series of appearances.

But how did Paul know? How did he know that there was such a series? Because it was in the tradition he had received, which as we have seen is much earlier than Luke's writing. But how did those early Christians who passed on the tradition to Paul and were the source of it know that the resurrection appearances formed a *series*? Because there must have been *a recognisable end*. They knew it was a series because the sequence had finished. It was no longer 'open'. But there must have been some special event that brought home to them that conviction. Luke says there was, and that event was the Ascension that occurred at Bethany on the slopes of the Mount of Olives (Luke 24.50; Acts 1.12). As John also refers to the Ascension (John 20.17), quite independently of Luke, it seems perverse not to take it seriously.

If we do, we will therefore want to say that at least it served to convince the disciples that the appearances had ended. If we are going to emphasise the resurrection and exaltation of Jesus as one unity, these appearances to the disciples of Jesus in bodily form perhaps 'were condescensions of the glorified Christ'. But whatever they were, they had ended. Jesus Christ had returned to and remained at his Father's 'right hand'.

Details

In the Acts' account of the Ascension it is portrayed as a decisive and deliberate withdrawal from sight; and there was something gradual about the withdrawal. Perhaps here is the problem. It was not an immediate disappearance. It was not like the disappearance of Christ on the Emmaus Road. On that occasion we are told, 'their eyes were opened and they recognised him; and he vanished out of their sight' (Luke 24.31).

Modern people, if they believe at all, probably find this sort of 'vanishing' more conceivable. They know the world of space and time; perhaps they can believe in the world of eternity and of the spirit at the same time. But the two are quite separate. So they find it easier to think of a sudden transition from time to eternity, with no connection and no merging of the two. It is easier to think of that than of time and eternity merging. Here is how C. S. Lewis explains it: 'Perhaps mere instantaneous vanishing would make us most comfortable. A sudden break between the perceptible and the imperceptible would worry us less than any kind of joint. But if the spectators say they saw first a short vertical movement and then a vague luminosity (that is what 'cloud' presumably means here as it certainly does in the account of the Transfiguration) and then nothing – have we any reason to object?'[7]

The 'cloud' was in the Bible a symbol often for the divine presence. In the days of Moses a 'cloud' was above the tent of meeting. It was a visible sign to Israel that the glory of the Lord was there (Exod. 40.34). A 'cloud' featured in the transfiguration of Jesus: 'a cloud overshadowed them' (Mark 9.7). And Jesus described his own return, his *parousia*, as a 'coming in clouds' (Mark 13.26; 14.62). That is why it is helpful to think of the transfiguration, ascension and *parousia* of Jesus as three successive manifestations to men of his divine glory.

Of course, there is a danger of pressing too far the details of an event like the Ascension. But according to Luke and Acts what happened was this: the disciples had an amazing and overwhelming experience of Christ as he decisively passed into a world beyond human conception and understanding; and those who spoke about it tried to tell the story in simple and intelligible words. They were forced to use what E. M. Blaiklock calls the 'symbols of wealth, royalty and elevation.'[8]

We need not be too concerned with the alleged 'three decker' theory of the universe that is said to make the account irrelevant if not fictitious. 'Anyone appearing to leave the earth's surface,' writes F. F. Bruce, 'must appear to spectators to be ascending, and so, when the cloud enveloped the visible form of their Lord, his disciples stood "looking steadfastly into heaven as he went." Some of them, perhaps, remembering a previous experience, expected that the cloud would dissolve and Jesus be left with them, as on the mount of transfiguration.'[9]

We cannot press the details too far. But we can understand that the Ascension is speaking of a link between time and eternity. It all ties in with the empty tomb. If the tomb was empty on that first resurrection morning, as we have suggested it was, Jesus had a resurrection body, a glorified body – a body 'raised in glory' (1 Cor. 15.43). It was not a crude resuscitation of a corpse. It was not the putting together of the pre-crucifixion body of Jesus. It was a transformed body. It was the body of the new age, the resurrection age. Yet it was not unrelated to the old body. It all adds up to this. Eternity is not unrelated to this world of space and time. We can't just separate time and eternity, or matter and spirit.

The incarnation spells this out. Then 'the Word became flesh' (John 1.14). The Ascension tells the same story. Time and eternity *are* connected. This is also what Peter is concerned to say in his first epistle. He believed that the affairs of space and time can and are affected by real ties with 'heaven'. The sufferings he and his friends were going through were not happening in a vacuum. They were not a piece of blind fate alone. They were certainly not out of control.

'At the right hand of God'

The Ascension, the New Testament affirms, was an event in the past. Its ultimate importance, however, is not in itself and the details of it, nor even in the fact that it made the disciples aware that the resurrection appearances had ended. Its importance lies in what it then came to symbolise – the fact that Christ is now 'at the right hand of God.'

This is the best language can do. We have already noted the limitations of language and Augustine's comment on this phrase. Calvin quaintly puts it like this: 'It is not a question of the disposition of his body, but of the majesty of his authority.' Karl Barth says: 'It states pictorially the truth which from its very nature cannot be represented, that the might and sovereignty of God is in actual fact identical with the might and sovereignty of him who as true God became true man and as such died upon the cross and of course rose again.'[10] This is a picture of an Eastern court. It means that Christ is invested with the full majesty and authority of God.

This imagery did communicate, and it still does (we talk of 'the right hand man'). The early Christians communicated with it their supreme belief that *Jesus is reigning*. This was their basic belief about Christ.

They used to look back to the Old Testament to see verses or parts of the Old Testament that most applied to Jesus Christ and their experience of him in the present. There was one verse they went back to time and time again. What was it? It was the first verse of Psalm 110: 'The Lord says to my lord: "Sit at my right hand, till I make your enemies your footstool." '

Jesus himself had been the first one to use this text. According to Mark chapter 12 verse 36 he had done so in his teaching in the temple. Then at Pentecost Peter applied this verse to Jesus as the one 'exalted at the right hand of God' (Acts 2.33). It is cited in a number of places in the New Testament. As C. H. Dodd put it: 'Wherever we read of Christ being at the right hand of God, or of hostile powers being subjected to Him, the ultimate reference is to this passage. In view of the place which Psalm 110.1 holds in the New Testament, we may safely put it down as one of the fundamental texts of the primitive *kerygma*.'[11]

The use, then, of this imagery did not come about because of a particular view of the cosmos – a three decker view; rather it came about because the imagery was in the Old Testament. But more fundamental still, it came about because the early Christians believed it was profoundly true, Jesus *is* King.

Some think that it got into credal statements right from the start. Paul's letter to the Romans perhaps indicates this. At one point in that great epistle his argument presupposes that his readers know already that it is 'Christ Jesus who died, yes, who was raised from the dead, who is at the right hand of God, who indeed intercedes for us' (Rom. 8.34). Some think this reflects an early credal formula.

The idea was certainly central to the thinking of the writer of the epistle to the Hebrews. We are there told that Jesus was a 'high priest after the order of Melchizedek' (Heb. 5.10). Later he is said to be such a priest 'for ever' (Heb. 6.20). What was so significant about Melchizedek? He was both '*king* of Salem (Jerusalem)' and '*priest* of the Most High God' (Heb. 7.1). 'He is first, by translation of his name, king of righteousness, and then he is also king of Salem, that is, king of peace' (Heb. 7.2). Hebrews therefore stresses the kingship of Christ in his priestly role.

But perhaps the greatest statement of this theme is in the epistle to the Ephesians. Paul is wanting the Christians he is writing to to experience something of the power of God in their daily lives as they face the pressures of a hostile world. He also wants the Church to have a vision for what it is and what it can do. So he prays that they may know 'what is the immeasurable greatness of (God's) power in us who believe, according to the working of his great might which he accomplished in Christ when he raised him from the dead and made him sit at his right hand in the heavenly places, far above all rule and authority and power and dominion, and above every name that is named not only in this age but also in that which is to come; and he has put all things under his feet and has made him the head over all things for the church, which is his body, the fullness of him who fills all in all' (Eph. 1.19–23).

'Angels, authorities, and powers subject to him'

In the verse from 1 Peter that we have been looking at, we are told that 'angels, authorities, and powers' are now subject to

Christ. In Ephesians we are told that Christ is 'far above all rule and authority and power and dominion, and above every name that is named'. What are these 'authorities' and 'powers'? Are they the structures of society, as some say; or are they actual political rulers; or are they demonic forces behind both the structures and the rulers?

There has been much debate over these questions. Michael Green reminds us of 'the flexibility of such terms as "principalities" and "powers" in the usage of the New Testament. They do, on occasion, refer to human authorities. They do, for the main part, refer to super human agencies in the spiritual world.'[12]

The New Testament clearly believes in 'the Devil' – 'the slanderer'. It implies that the evil in the world is not to be accounted for by the sum total of individual misdeeds. There is an 'extra'. And the Bible encourages us to think of that 'extra' in personal terms – a 'he', not an 'it'. But the Devil can then be seen to be steering other more neutral forces.

Therefore whatever the precise interpretation of 'authorities' and 'powers' is, we shall not go far wrong if we say this: that all demonic forces, all political forces, all economic forces, all sociological forces, all natural forces, indeed 'every name that is named', are subject to Christ. Jesus is 'far above all'. That was the New Testament's unshakable conviction. *Nothing* could or can thwart the purposes of Christ. This in turn gave and still gives wonderful hope and assurance.

'Who', asks Paul, 'shall separate us from the love of Christ? Shall tribulation, or distress, or persecution, or famine, or nakedness, or peril, or sword . . . ? No, in all these things we are more than conquerors through him who loved us. For I am sure that neither death, nor life, nor angels, nor principalities, nor things present, nor things to come, nor powers, nor height, nor depth, nor anything else in all creation, will be able to separate us from the love of God in Christ Jesus our Lord' (Rom. 8.35, 37–9).

Conclusion

Where did Jesus go? As we say in the Apostles' Creed: 'I believe . . . He descended to the dead. On the third day he rose again. He ascended into heaven, and is seated at the right hand of the

Father'. Millions of Christians in the last decades of the twentieth century believe that this is the central fact of existence – the resurrection of Jesus. Their concern is that more should know it and live in the light of it.

Epilogue

Paul was in Athens. He was preaching before a very sophisticated audience about the resurrection of Jesus Christ from the dead. What was their reaction? Exactly the same reaction as people today have to the message of the Resurrection. 'Now when they heard of the resurrection of the dead, some mocked; but others said, "We will hear you again about this." . . . But some men joined him and believed' (Acts 17.32, 34).

There were and are three reactions: some mock, others want to know more, some join and believe.

Some mock

There have always been those who have mocked the gospel of Jesus and his resurrection. We mentioned Voltaire in the Introduction, the eighteenth-century Frenchman. The eighteenth century could be called the 'classical age of mockery'. Another Frenchman, Montesquieu, after a visit to England at that time reported: 'there is no religion, and the subject, if mentioned in Society, excites nothing but laughter.'

But remember what then happened in eighteenth-century England. Two brothers by the name of Wesley went up to the University of Oxford. There they met with friends for prayer, bible study and discussion. In the end God dealt in an amazing way with members of that group. One day John Wesley's heart was 'strangely warmed', as for the first time he understood something of the love and goodness of God who had raised Jesus from the dead. The same thing was to happen to a thoroughly godless young man at the University of Cambridge, Charles Simeon; when he was obliged to attend King's College Chapel, he began to think. The result? On Easter day, 1779, he woke up in the morning with the words ringing in his mind: 'Jesus Christ is risen today! Hallelujah.' He tells us: 'from that hour peace flowed in rich abundance into my soul.'

The result of all this was the Evangelical revival. And the course of English history and, through the consequent missionary movement, world history was affected. When the Evangelical revival produced men like Wilberforce and his opposition to slavery, English society no longer could laugh and mock at the gospel of the resurrection of Jesus Christ. It had, rather, to weep at the inhumanity the gospel was exposing.

Others want to know more

What about those who want to know more? This class is increasing in the Western World as the twentieth century is drawing to a close. This is coinciding with the loss of confidence in science and technology we spoke about in the first chapter. Although technology frees man from so much hardship, 'it threatens,' says Jerome Wiesner, a Provost of the Massachusetts Institute of Technology, 'to dehumanise him more completely than the often uneven struggle of earlier times.' And as it does so, twentieth-century technological man is ceasing to mock and is wanting to hear more about Jesus and the Resurrection.

Some want to hear more because they genuinely want to discover more. Others want to hear more because they want to put off the time when they should commit themselves to the risen Jesus, as a person. But we need to make that commitment to discover the truth of the Resurrection. If we enter into a relationship with him, we find that he is risen and ascended. We then know he has gone 'to the right hand of God' and now reigns.

Some join and believe

But how do you do that? How do you begin such a relationship? After preaching his Pentecost sermon, and telling of the resurrection and exaltation of Christ, there were those who said to Peter, 'What shall we do?' (Acts 2.37). And his reply to them was, 'Repent, and be baptized every one of you in the name of Jesus

Christ for the forgiveness of your sins; and you shall receive the gift of the Holy Spirit' (Acts 2.38).

You have to *repent*. That means you have to 'think again' or 'rethink' – that is what the original word in the Greek means. You have to think again about Jesus Christ, yourself and your sin. And that is often, if not always, humbling.

You have to see Jesus as Lord. You realise that he and the Father are one, and that he is the one to whom we rightly say 'My Lord and my God' (John 20.28). As Paul says, Jesus Christ our Lord was 'designated Son *of God* in power according to the Spirit of holiness by his resurrection from the dead' (Rom. 1.4). The Resurrection points to his deity.

But besides admitting, you need to submit to his Lordship. That means you have to say 'No' to your sin and selfishness; and that is often hard.

You have to be *baptised*; or if you have been baptised already and it has meant little to you, you ought to take some other public step to prove that your rethinking is real – even if it is just telling a Christian friend. Baptism is 'for the forgiveness of your sins'. If you believe, you will realise that on the cross Jesus Christ died for you in your place, so that you might be free. The Resurrection was God's 'Yes' to the cross. This is a mystery, but in Christ we can all be accepted by God even though we are still very imperfect. God accepts us just as we are. We don't first have to impress God. That is the gospel. He loves us with all our sin, guilt and failings; being accepted we can *then*, from a position of strength, begin to live for him. And we do that in the fellowship of the Church. Baptism is the 'badge' of Church membership. We must regularly meet with other Christians, if we believe. As happened in Athens, the believers 'joined' up with Paul.

And so if we believe, we are to *receive the gift of the Holy Spirit*. Jesus said: 'It is to your advantage that *I go away*, for if I do not go away, the Counsellor will not come to you; but if I go, I will send him to you' (John 16.7). As we open our lives to the Holy Spirit, so we come to know the risen Jesus even more. What do we need the Holy Spirit for? To make us more like Jesus himself. He 'sanctifies the people of God'. But he also strengthens us and helps us to witness to the resurrection of Jesus ourselves. *We* are to go out into all the world to witness and by his Holy Spirit Jesus Christ is with us as we do so.

After his resurrection Jesus told his disciples: 'Go therefore and make disciples of all nations, baptizing them in the name of the Father and of the Son and of the Holy Spirit, teaching them to observe all that I have commanded you; and lo, *I am with you always, to the close of the age*' (Matt. 28.19–20). As we go, so he goes.

Where did Jesus go? To the Father. But through us, in the power of his Holy Spirit, he can now go out into the world. St Theresa of Avila once said: 'Christ has no body now on earth but yours; no hands but yours; no feet but yours; yours are the eyes through which is to look out Christ's compassion to the world; yours are the feet through which he is to go about doing good; yours are the hands with which he is to bless men now.'

Notes

Chapter 1: Miracles, science and the modern world

1. G. R. Beasley-Murray, *Christ is Alive* (Lutterworth Press, London, 1947), p. 29.
2. reported in *The Observer*, 2nd June, 1974.
3. David Hume, *An Enquiry Concerning Human Understanding* Section X (of Miracles), part 1 (The Open Court Publishing Co., Chicago, 1907), p. 120.
4. Christopher Booker, *The Seventies – portrait of a decade* (Allen Lane, London, 1980), p. 23.
5. Michael Talbot, *Mysticism and the New Physics* (Bantam Books, New York, 1981), p. 42.
6. James Martin, *Did Jesus Rise from the Dead?* (Lutterworth Press, London, 1956), p. 13.
7. C. F. von Weizsäcker, *The Relevance of Science – creation and cosmogeny* (Collins, London, 1964), p. 22.
8. M. A. H. Melinsky, *Healing Miracles* (A. R. Mowbray, London, 1968), p. 59.
9. Plutarch, *Pyrrhus* xxi 3.
10. C. F. D. Moule, *Miracles – Cambridge studies in their Philosophy and History* (A. R. Mowbray, London, 1968), p. 16.
11. cited by M. A. H. Melinsky, op. cit., p. 4.

Chapter 2: The issues involved

1. Bertrand Russell, *Autobiography* (George Allen and Unwin, London, 1968), vol. 2, p. 156.
2. ibid., p. 158.
3. Josephus, *Antiq.* 18. i. 3.
4. B. Layton, *The Gnostic Treatise on Resurrection from Nag Hammadi, Edited, with Translation and Commentary* (Scholars Press, Missoula, 1979), 48.6, p. 27.

5. J. B. Phillips, *Ring of Truth* (Hodder and Stoughton, London, 1967), p. 7.

6. G. W. H. Lampe in *The Resurrection – a dialogue arising from broadcasts by G. W. H. Lampe and D. M. MacKinnon*, ed. William Purcell (A. R. Mowbray, London, 1966), p. 8.

7. ibid., p. 17.

8. P. F. Strawson, *Individuals – an Essay in Descriptive Metaphysics* (Methuen, London, 1959), p. 116.

9. quoted by D. S. Cairns, *The Reasonableness of the Christian Faith* (Hodder and Stoughton, London, 1918), p. 153.

10. C. F. D. Moule, *The significance of the Message of the Resurrection for Faith in Jesus Christ* (SCM Press, London, 1968), p. 9.

11. Merrill C. Tenney, 'The Historicity of the Resurrection' in *Jesus of Nazareth: Saviour and Lord*, ed. Carl F. H. Henry (Tyndale Press, London, 1970), p. 143.

12. G. E. Ladd, *I believe in the Resurrection of Jesus* (Hodder and Stoughton, London, 1975), p. 126.

Chapter 3: The shape of history

1. Paul Minear, *To die and to live: Christ's resurrection and Christian vocation* (Seabury Press, New York, 1977), p. 53.

2. Herbert Butterfield, *Christianity and History* (Collins, London, 1957), p. 39.

3. Marx and Engels, *The Communist Manifesto*, ed. A. J. P. Taylor (Penguin Books, London, 1967), p. 79.

4. Proclus, *Procli Diodocli in Platonis Timaeum Commentaria* 3.30.

5. John Baillie, *Invitation to Pilgrimage* (Penguin Books, London, 1960), p. 103.

6. G. E. Ladd, *A Theology of the New Testament* (Lutterworth Press, Guildford, 1975), p. 316.

Chapter 4: 'In accordance with the Scriptures'

1. S. H. Hooke, *The Resurrection of Christ as history and experience* (Darton, Longman and Todd, London, 1967), p. 8.

2. Donald Guthrie, *New Testament Theology* (Inter-Varsity Press, Leicester, 1981), p. 376ff.

3. D. E. Jenkins and G. B. Caird, *Jesus and God* (Faith Press, London, 1965), p. 17.

4. E. Hennecke, *New Testament Apocrypha* (SCM Press, London, 1963), vol. 1, p. 186.

5. Frank Morison, *Who Moved the Stone?* (Faber, London, 1930), p. 5.

6. James Martin, *Did Jesus Rise . . . ?* op. cit., p. 40.

7. Leon Morris, *Luke* (Inter-Varsity Press, London, 1974), p. 333ff.

8. Michael Green, *The Day Death Died* (Inter-Varsity Press, Leicester, 1982), p. 32.

9. G. R. Beasley-Murray, *Christ is Alive* op. cit., p. 18.

Chapter 5: Is it true?

1. Emil Brunner, *Our Faith* (SCM Press, London, 1949), p. 17.

2. F. F. Bruce, *Tradition Old and New* (Paternoster Press, Exeter, 1970), p. 40ff.

3. James Martin, *Did Jesus Rise . . . ?* op. cit., p. 25.

4. quoted by F. F. Bruce, op. cit., p. 41.

5. ibid. see p. 68ff.

6. James Martin, op. cit., p. 25.

7. F. F. Bruce, op. cit., p. 64ff.

8. C. H. Dodd, *The Founder of Christianity* (Macmillan, New York, 1970), p. 164.

9. D. L. Sayers, *The Man Born to be King* (Gollancz, London, 1943), p. 33.

10. A. N. Sherwin-White, *Roman Society and Roman Law in the New Testament* (Oxford University Press, 1973).

11. G. B. Caird, *Saint Luke* (Penguin Books, London, 1963), p. 29.

12. *The Times*, 11th May, 1974 and my reply 17th May, 1974.

13. R. T. France, 'The Authenticity of the Sayings of Jesus', in *History, Criticism and Faith*, ed. Colin Brown (Inter-Varsity Press, Leicester, 1976), p. 129.

Chapter 6: 'The one disconcerting fact'

1. Gilbert West, *Observations on the History and Evidence of the Resurrection of Jesus Christ* (R. Dodsley, London, 1747), p. vii.

2. C. F. D. Moule, *The Phenomenon of the New Testament* (SCM Press, London, 1967), p. 2.

3. Tertullian, *De Spectaculis* 30, cited by Robert H. Stein, 'Was the tomb really empty?' *Themelios*, vol. 5, no. 1 (September 1979), p. 9.

4. C. H. Dodd, *The Founder* . . . op cit., p. 166.

5. D. M. Mackinnon, in *The Resurrection* . . . op. cit., p. 84.

6. *The Observer*, 22nd April, 1973.

7. C. H. Dodd, op. cit., p. 166.

8. see Robert H. Stein, op. cit., p. 10.

9. D. F. Strauss, *New Life of Jesus* (Williams and Norgate, London, 1865), vol. 1, p. 412.

10. Hugh J. Schonfield, *The Passover Plot* (Bantam Books, New York, 1967), 22nd printing, September 1978.

11. J. N. D. Anderson, *Christianity: The Witness of History* (Tyndale Press, London, 1969), p. 65.

12. Frank Morison, *Who Moved . . . ?* op. cit., p. 33.

13. G. R. Beasley-Murray, *Christ is Alive*, op. cit., p. 33.

14. quoted by Frank Morison, op. cit., p. 98.

15. C. H. Dodd, op. cit., p. 181.

16. ibid. p. 170.

17. H. L. A. Hart, *Definition and Theory in Jurisprudence* (Oxford University Press, 1953), p. 14.

18. J. L. Austin, Philosophical Papers, ed. J. O. Urmson and G. J. Warnock (Oxford University Press, 1961), p. 36.

19. D. M. Baillie, *God was in Christ* (Faber, London, 1961), p. 109.

Chapter 7: Just a dream?

1. C. F. D. Moule and Don Cupitt, 'The Resurrection: A Disagreement', *Theology*, vol. LXXV No. 628 (October 1972), p. 509.

2. C. M. Deasy, *Design for Human Affairs* (Wiley, New York, 1974), p. 45.

3. C. F. D. Moule, *The Significance* . . . op. cit., p. 4.

4. G. E. Ladd, *I believe* . . . op. cit., p. 36.

5. Michael Green, *The Day Death Died*, op. cit., p. 43ff.

6. James Martin, *Did Jesus Rise . . . ?* op. cit., p. 91.

Chapter 8: The Church of Jesus Christ

1. C. Peter Wagner, *Stop the World I want to get on* (Regal Books, Glendale, 1974), p. 7.

2. statistics from the Missions Advanced Research and Communication Centre, Monrovia, California, USA. Other statistics can be found in David B. Barrett, *World Christian Encylopaedia* (Oxford University Press, 1982).

3. C. Peter Wagner, op. cit., p. 10.

4. ibid., p. 2.

5. James Martin, *Did Jesus Rise . . . ?* op. cit., p. 77.

6. Christopher Dawson, *The Historic Reality of Christian Culture* (Routledge and Kegan Paul, London, 1960), p. 15.

7. Ignatius, *Magnesians* 9.

8. *Didache* 14.

9. C. F. D. Moule and Don Cupitt, *Theology* (October 1972), op. cit., p. 513.

10. John R. W. Stott, *What Christ Thinks of the Church* (Lutterworth Press, London, 1958), p. 39.

11. ibid., p. 41, *The Martyrdom of Polycarp*, 9 and 14.

Chapter 9: Belief and doubt

1. quoted by G. E. Ladd, *I believe . . .* op. cit., p. 26.

2. quoted by Albert J. Wollen, *How to Conduct Home Bible Classes* (Scripture Press, Wheaton, 1969), p. 8.

3. C. S. Lewis, *Mere Christianity* (Collins, London, 1955), p. 122.

4. Charles Darwin, *The Autobiography* (Dover, New York, 1958), p. 62.

5. C. S. Lewis, *The Screwtape Letters* (Geoffrey Bles, London, 1942), p. 65.

6. Os Guinness, *Doubt* (Lion Publishing, Berkhamsted, 1976), p. 72.

7. Michael Green, *Jesus Spells Freedom* (Inter-Varsity Press, London, 1972), p. 72.

8. quoted by Os Guiness, op. cit., p. 102.

9. E. Frank, *Philosophical Understanding and Religious Truth* (Oxford University Press, 1945), p. 40.

10. Sir Frederick Catherwood, *A better way* (Inter-Varsity Press, London, 1975), p. 49.

11. *The Sunday Times*, 27th December, 1981.

12. David Watson, *I Believe in Evangelism* (Hodder and Stoughton, London, 1976), p. 101.

13. Carl Jung, *Modern Man in Search of a Soul* (Harcourt, Brace and World, New York, 1933), p. 229.

14. reported by Hubert J. Richards, *The First Easter: What really happened?* (Collins, London, 1976), p. 67.

15. Michael Green, *Runaway World* (Inter-Varsity Press, London, 1968), p. 36.

16. Karl Barth, 'Evangelical Theology in the 19th Century', *Scottish Journal of Theology Occasional Papers, 8* (Oliver and Boyd, Edinburgh, 1959), p. 58.

Chapter 10: Where did Jesus go? – 'to the dead'

1. in *Absurd Drama*, ed. Martin Esslin (Penguin Books, London, 1965), pp. 25–116.

2. quoted by C. E. B. Cranfield, *I & II Peter and Jude* (SCM Press, London, 1960), p. 104.

3. R. Bultmann, *Kerygma and Myth*, ed. H. W. Bartsch (SPCK, London, 1953), vol. 1, p. 10.

4. Augustine, *On Faith and the Creed*, Works of Augustine (T & T Clark, Edinburgh, 1873), vol. 9, p. 356.

5. J. I. Packer, *I want to be a Christian* (Kingsway Publications, Eastbourne, 1977), p. 49.

6. C. E. B. Cranfield, op. cit., p. 104.

7. F. F. Bruce, *St Matthew* (Scripture Union, London, 1970), p. 92.

8. A. Plummer, *An Exegetical Commentary on the Gospel according to St Matthew* (Elliot Stock, London, 1909), p. 402.

9. Ovid, *Metamorphoses* Book VII, tr. Mary M. Innes (Penguin Books, London, 1955), p. 171ff.

10. A. Plummer, op. cit., p. 402.

11. E. Hennecke, *New Testament Apocrypha*, vol. 1, op. cit., p. 470.

12. F. F. Bruce, op. cit., p. 92.

Chapter 11: Where did Jesus go? – 'to prepare a place'

1. BBC 2 *Newsnight*, 25th February, 1982.

2. reported by John Lewis, 'The Spirit in the religious life', *Bishop's Move*, ed. Michael Harper (Hodder and Stoughton, London, 1978), p. 113.

3. John R. W. Stott, *Christ the Liberator* (Inter-Varsity Press, Downers Grove, 1971), p. 32ff.

4. ibid., p. 34. Here John Stott shows that the 'intermediate' and 'final' state are to be seen as being 'with Christ'. I have reflected his thinking in the next paragraph.

5. see John Baillie, *And the Life Everlasting* (Epworth Press, London, 1961), p. 153.

6. Murray Harris, 'Resurrection and immortality: eight theses', *Themelios*, vol. 1, No. 2 (Spring 1976), p. 52.

7. C. K. Barrett, 'Immortality and Resurrection' in *Resurrection and Immortality*, ed. Charles S. Duthie (Bagster, London, 1979), p. 87.

8. Lesslie Newbigin, *The Finality of Christ* (SCM Press, London, 1969), p. 50.

9. G. R. Driver, *Canaanite Myths and Legends* (T & T Clark, Edinburgh, 1956), p. 72ff.

10. James B. Pritchard, *The Ancient Near East – an Anthology of Texts and Pictures* (Princeton University Press, 1978), p. 40.

11. Apuleius, *The Golden Ass*, tr. Robert Graves (Penguin Books, London, 1950), p. 286.

12. J. N. D. Anderson, *Christianity and Comparative Religion* (Tyndale Press, London, 1970), p. 38.

13. James Orr, *The Resurrection of Jesus* (Hodder and Stoughton, London, 1908), p. 146.

14. David Watson, *Is Any One There?* (Hodder and Stoughton, London, 1979), p. 87.

Chapter 12: Where did Jesus go? – 'to the right hand of God'

1. John A. T. Robinson, *Honest to God* (SCM Press, London, 1963), p. 11.

2. C. J. Cadoux, *The Historic Mission of Jesus* (Lutterworth Press, London, 1941), p. 284.

3. G. R. Beasley-Murray, *Christ is Alive*, op. cit., p. 150.

4. Basil of Cappadocia, *Hexaëmeron* Homily I. 2.

5. G. E. Ladd, *A Theology* . . . op. cit., p. 334.

6. A. M. Ramsey, *The Resurrection of Christ* (Collins, London, 1961), p. 123.

7. C. S. Lewis, *Miracles* (Collins, London, 1960), p. 160.

8. E. M. Blaiklock, *The Acts of the Apostles* (Tyndale Press, London, 1959), p. 51.

9. F. F. Bruce, *The Book of Acts* (Marshall, Morgan and Scott, London, 1962), p. 41.

10. Karl Barth, *Credo*, tr. J. S. McNab (Hodder and Stoughton, London, 1936), p. 106.

11. C. H. Dodd, *The Apostolic Preaching and its Developments* (Hodder and Stoughton, London, 1963), p. 15.

12. Michael Green, *I believe in Satan's Downfall* (Hodder and Stoughton, London, 1981), p. 86.